From Ruff to Riches

Emily Buhrow

RAINBOW ZOO PUBLISHING

Rainbow Zoo Publishing

Paperback ISBN: 978-1-950476-66-4

ebook ISBN: 978-1-950476-67-1

To my first rescue dog, Beau, the one who started it all.

Contents

Fast Facts about Fostering

- Fostering saves lives. (Both of humans and animals.)

- It is the most effective way to reduce unnecessary euthanasia and overcrowding in rescues.

- It saves the lives of the most vulnerable animals, like kittens and puppies who are more susceptible to picking up diseases in a rescue setting.

- Injured animals heal better in a comfortable environment, like a foster home, with significantly less stress.

- According to an article from NIH News in Health, "The Power of Pets: Health Benefits of Human-Animal Interactions," fostering and adopting an animal can improve your physical and mental health; interacting with animals has been shown to decrease stress and lower blood pressure. This interaction can also reduce loneliness, increase feelings of social support, and boost your mood. Having a dog to walk can encourage you to walk more, benefiting your physical health.

- It's mostly if not completely free, depending on how the rescue operates and what they provide.

- You can pick which animal you want to foster!

- You can foster as much, or as little, as you want.

Foreword

By Stephanie Buhrow

What do you do when your wife asks you to write the foreword for her book? You put it off of course! But I have been gently reminded to get started at least four times now, so with my coffee in hand and three dogs snuggled around me, I guess I should start.

Emily and I met in college at Illinois Wesleyan University. We had mutual friends and often ran into each other at weekend outings. Finding a common interest in quoting the movie *Bridesmaids*, we started spending more and more time together. I don't think either of us had any idea what lay ahead for us, but it did not take long before animals became a big part of it.

A little over six months after we started dating, Emily adopted her first rescue dog, Beau. Fast forward a handful of months, Emily had her first foster dog, Rex. She continued to foster whenever possible while living in different apartments and rental units, but when we moved into our house in 2018, fostering became one of our shared passions.

Emily is the kind of person you can't sum up in just a few words because there are too many good things about her. Saying she is kind doesn't cover how deeply giving, considerate, and loving she is. She puts others (furry and human) first and is constantly looking to better the lives of those around her. Whether it be something big, like organizing a Christmas gift drive for residents in senior living facilities to make their Christmas wishes come true, or something small, like buying formula for someone who can't afford to buy more, Emily is always trying to better her community. Fostering animals is just one of those many ways she makes the world a better place.

Emily is many things. She is a caring daughter and sister, dedicated friend, unofficial life coach, talented three-point shooter, and a master of remembering quotes from comedy movies. For the record, seeing her achieve her dream of becoming a published author (and finally using her English degree) has been amazing, but watching her become a mother has been my favorite to date. It was such a natural transition because her caregiving characteristics and tendencies make her a great mother. After we came home from the hospital with Louie (our sweet baby boy, born in July 2022), she was amazing about telling me to go take a nap when I needed it but didn't realize it. She is caring, nurturing, gentle, and so in tune with what Louie needs and wants. Emily is the best at getting Louie to belly laugh and despite my doubts, has been easily getting up early to be with him (which is impressive, because my girl loves her sleep *a lot*).

Emily has this superpower to realize when someone needs help but isn't asking for it. If I am stressing over unfinished laundry I can't get to because I will be home late, it's already done when I get home. I forgot to scoop the litter box? No problem, she's got me covered (and this is important because we have a pup who enjoys what we call "litter box treats"). She can sense when I'm too tired to cook dinner, and she'll suggest ordering out before I have to say it.

Her amazing, kind-hearted spirit does not stop with humans. I can't tell you how many times I've gotten a text from her about a sad, scared, and underfed animal that needs our help. (You'll see what I'm talking about.)

It isn't just the fostering that makes her amazing though. She puts out cat shelters in the winter to keep animals warm who need it. We not only have bird feeders in our back yard, but we also have a "Squirrel Saloon" to offer snacks and shelters to squirrels too. She uses her writing skills and creativity to create bios and descriptions for adoptable animals that are fun and effective. She donates pet food and supplies to community members who are unable to provide for their pets. She has even helped someone who adopted one of our fosters to cover veterinary expenses. Her compassion knows no limits.

Another important thing to know about Emily... her sense of humor is outrageous. I have never in my life laughed as hard as I do when I am with her. She is amazing at coming up with puns. I probably shouldn't divulge this, but she has me challenge her by giving her random words or objects and she'll create a pun about it. She has a sharp wit and when you really get to know her, you'll see just how weird and silly she is. I guarantee if you talk to anyone who knows Emily, one of the first things they'll say about her is how filled with joy and humor she is.

Emily is about to share her story and how she found the joys of animal rescue. You will meet all our fosters. Some were brief stays, some we had for a while, some we lost unexpectedly, and some never left, but all were loved and touched our lives in one way or another. You may cry, maybe you'll even feel inspired. You will likely learn something new about fostering animals. What I know for certain is you will be entertained, and you will laugh, whether it is with us or at us – doesn't matter. Emily's kind heart, and passion for helping others are evident in her writing, as she guides you through her fostering journey. Every journey has a beginning, and hers begins with Beau.

Meet Beau Bear

On January 20, 2014, I woke up to rain drops on my window and an empty, quiet house. My college roommates were at basketball practice. Usually, I would be there with them, but I quit the Illinois Wesleyan University basketball team a few days earlier due to a back injury I did not have the motivation to make a "comeback" from. Feeling lonely, sad, and slightly depressed, I started scrolling animal rescue websites looking for adoptable dogs.

The thought of adopting a dog had been in the back of my mind since my sister, Molly, started volunteering at Illinois Valley Animal Rescue (IVAR). As she described the homeless dogs there, the desire to save one of them grew in my heart.

Amidst my scrolling, I came across this one-year-old Beagle mix with the most soulful eyes. Brown and white coloring with a voluptuous fluffy tail, Beau drew me in right away. He looked lonely, sad, and slightly depressed. Sound familiar? We needed each other. If I connected with him like this through a computer screen, imagine the connection we would have in person.

As I proceeded to fall in love, my "logical" thinking took over my mind. *I'm just a college student. Is this a stupid, irresponsible decision? Am I around enough to take care of a dog? Am I acting on impulse?*

Doubt filled my mind. I had very little experience with caring for a dog. My family had a few pets growing up—a cat named Jingles and a yorkie named Josie—but being involved in sports and kind of a selfish teenager, then going off to college, I can't say I had a super strong bond with them. Adopting a dog of my own would be my first true experience of life with a pet, especially because I couldn't rely on my mom to feed and take care of it. Panic.

It brought me some peace knowing Molly volunteered at the rescue Beau stayed at. She answered my questions as I tried to figure it out and come down from my panic attack. Without her I don't think I would've gone through with it.

She explained he arrived at the rescue with his brother Buzz, who she noticed picked on him a little. Beau didn't stick up for himself when being picked on either, which broke my heart. I also had a passive personality and didn't always stick up for myself, so this characteristic of his spoke to me. He needed me to bust him out. I made up my mind and hit "submit" on Beau's application.

A few days later, I was on my way to meet Beau. My heart and mind raced as I stepped into the rescue. As I walk down the "hallway" of dog cages, I was greeted with loud barks and howls and the nose-scrunching smell of dogs. I had no idea so many dogs needed homes. This first experience of an animal rescue began to change my perspective on life and rescue animals. *What an incredible operation!*

All the dogs have the essentials they need: food, water, bed, toys, etc. They are surely better off here than on the streets, but they still need a place and a family to call their own.

About five cages down on my right, I saw the sweetest face looking back at me: my Beau Bear! A confirmed love-at-first-sight encounter, or second sight, if you count me seeing his pictures online. Much to my surprise, his pictures made him look smaller than his actual size. I anticipated a thirty-pound dog, but he weighed closer to fifty pounds. Still, when my mind is made up, I'm determined to make it work. Molly let him out of his cage and took him into the yard. As I approached him, he didn't know what to think of me. I don't blame him. I'm sure he thought something like, *who is this crazy lady baby talking to me? Get out of my way, I really need to pee.*

After a long tinkle in the yard, he came up to me for a sniff or two, trying to figure me out. I offered him a few treats and pets, but for the most part he kept his distance. He did accept a treat though; that's when I first learned where Beau's heart lied...with food. I let the rescue director know I would love to move forward with the adoption, but she seemed hesitant to let me adopt him since I was a junior in college, renting a house, etc. My anger and impatience were at the forefront of my emotions, but as I calmed down, I understood why she needed to be cautious. Her job is to make sure these dogs get adopted and stay adopted, so she needed to feel confident about Beau's placement.

Molly and I left the rescue after visiting Beau, and I anxiously awaited a return call from the director to hear if my application would be approved and if or when I could bring Beau home with me. During this anxiety-ridden waiting period, I went to a local bagel shop for lunch (despite my lack of appetite with my stomach in knots). Molly and I talked at the counter about Beau as we ordered, and it turns out, the owner of the bagel shop who knew my family and me, also knew the rescue director very well. *Serendipity!* She so kindly put in a good word for me, and I got the call that Beau would be mine.

A couple Sundays later, Super Bowl Sunday 2014 to be exact, is one of the best days of my life: Adoption Day! I went to PetSmart with Molly to pick out a crate, collar, food bowls, and a leash. We picked Beau up at the rescue and the battle to get him into the back seat of the car began. Other onlookers who witnessed this battle likely suspected we were kidnapping him due to his persistent unwillingness to move from the ground. We eventually convinced him we were not abductors and got him in the car. (I picked him up and had to lovingly shove him in there butt first.)

Beau knew Molly a bit more than me, which I thought would help with the transition, but he was terrified; panting, shaking, and side-eyeing me the whole way. I sat in the back seat with him as his shedding white hair created a snow globe effect, and my arm around him went up and down with the rapid pace of his heartbeat. I tried to calm him down with soft words of reassurance but had no luck. Can you imagine being taken from place to place, meeting new people all the time, and now being in a car with strangers? Stressful.

Molly, Beau, and I made it to my parents' house about ten minutes later. We let him explore the back yard and take another potty break before Beau and I were off to my college house in Bloomington, IL. I obsessively checked on him in the rearview mirror to see if he settled at all. You'll pick up quickly that I'm an anxious Annie. The hour-long car ride felt like days, but we made it and began settling in at my house, where he met my roommates and my girlfriend (now wife) Stephanie.

Inspecting the yard, taking a walk, and eating his food were first on our agenda upon arrival. He marked about every blade of grass but had no accidents in the house, to my surprise. The rescue noted him as potty trained, which I've since learned can sometimes be inaccurate, but Beau definitely knew where and when to go potty. He's the best boy. Walking him down the street and around campus, we couldn't wipe the smiles off our faces. We both knew we'd found the perfect companion.

Escaping living in a cage and getting picked on by his brother, Beau began his new life. Beau calmed down and sat with me on the couch to watch the Super Bowl. I told him he didn't *have* to like sports in order to live here, but it sure would be cool if he did. No issues there, he's a big sports fan, just like me.

At bedtime, I put him in his crate. He whined for two or three minutes before I caved and let him sleep with me. He hasn't been in a crate since! Going to class the next day, my nerves took over as I left him in my room. I had no clue what he might do without supervision. I anxiously tapped my feet through my fifty-minute English class, paying little to no attention to the lecture. I couldn't wait to get back home to Beau! I arrived home to find him fast asleep on my bed like the great dog he is.

A small wrench in our newfound happiness occurred when Beau met my roommate's dog, Remi. Both my roommate and I had no idea how to introduce dogs to each other. We let them briefly meet outside then let them both in the house. Would. Not. Recommend. It is important dogs meet in a neutral territory for the first few encounters, and then slowly introduce them into the same home. Remi had lived there for a few weeks, so from her perspective, Beau invaded her space, and she got defensive. They did not fight, but definitely tried to. We separated them by using one of our couches and chairs to block the large doorway from the living room to the dining room. They tried to bark and growl at each other through the gaps in the furniture for a few days.

This caused everyone in the house tons of stress. *Should I have made sure Remi liked Beau before adopting him? Yep.* I've learned a lot about dogs throughout the years and sincerely wish younger me knew those things, but "gotta start somewhere," right? It became my top priority to get Beau and Remi to get along.

I walked them around the neighborhood together several times a day. One snowy February day I bundled up and got them ready for a walk. After about forty minutes, we walked through the back alley back to the house when a pesky squirrel popped out of nowhere and challenged Remi to a battle. Remi lifted off with all of her strength, pulling me face first into the snow, and took off after the squirrel. Beau stayed right next to me and asked (with his face), "Uh, mom, you ok? I think Remi went that way." *Thanks, Beau.*

I was able to catch her as she patiently waited at the bottom of the tree where the squirrel escaped to. Frozen-faced and not particularly happy, we all made it back home. It took at least a week of walking them together (and only one squirrel incident), but mission accomplished. Beau and Remi figured out how to cohabitate, and we could put our furniture back in its rightful place. I felt a weight lift off my shoulders when they became friends.

I took Beau to his very first veterinary appointment the following week, and he got a good report overall. The vet noted it felt as though his ribs may have been broken at some point and didn't heal properly based on what she felt during his physical exam. She didn't seem concerned about it and it didn't bother him, but I still didn't like knowing someone mistreated him in the past. I had not yet experienced any type of animal abuse firsthand in my life, thankfully. I knew there were many animals in rescues, but I never thought about how they ended up there.

Looking at Beau, I wondered how someone could be so mean to such an innocent creature and how incredible it is that he still trusts humans.

No wonder he feared Molly and me at first. He didn't know if he could trust us or not. I began to learn how forgiving dogs can be. They are the prime example of unconditional love. Feeling bad for him, Beau got several extra treats when we finished up at the vet. That's when I discovered his undying love for McDonald's vanilla ice cream. The crazed look in his eyes as he inhaled the ice cream made my day brighter. Speaking of treats, Beau got real chubby real fast. I gave him too many treats I'm sure, but as I figured out how to be a more responsible dog owner, we got that under control with a good diet and more walks around the neighborhood.

As Beau continued to become comfortable with me, more of his adorable personality began to shine. "Walk" and "eat" were the two main words in his vocabulary. His ears perk straight up, his mouth chomps the air, and his tail goes from zero to one hundred when I mention either of those words. His determination and patience for food are unmatched. Once he locks eyes with that piece of bread, I'm convinced he will wait several years to have a bite. Beau's favorite foods are, well, anything edible (besides lettuce; do not insult him with a piece of lettuce, *yuck*), but he's a big fan of lunch meat, carrots, and yogurt. The yogurt container looks brand new by the time he's done with it.

When it's time for a walk, the zoomies come out! He hauls butt around the house and yard as if I told him we are going to Disney World. He claims every fire hydrant and pole as his own by marking it with pee, even if it's just a dribble. No opportunity for marking must be left behind. If he knows we are close to home and the walk is ending, he intentionally slows down because he doesn't want it to be over. He's kind of a genius.

Beau's favorite place to visit is his Grandma and Grandpa's house. They have a huge yard with so much room to run! And it helps that Grandpa gives him all the cheese balls his little heart, and chubby gut, desire. When it's time to leave, he hides in one of the bedrooms. All I see is his head peeking around the corner like "Mom, do we have to go?" Once I catch him, I have to drag him out to the car and lift him into the back seat because he refuses to do it himself.

Since we're on the topic of Beau's dislikes, let's talk about baths. Beau.

Hates. Baths. When I say the word, his ears drop and his tail immediately tucks between his legs. He promptly breaks eye contact and walks away. I have to carry him into the bathroom. The entire time I'm bathing him, he looks as though he just received traumatic news. The drama! When I pick him up from the groomer, they say, "He did great, but he looks so sad." To which I respond, "I promise he's actually a very happy dog who has a great life."

My favorite part about Beau is his snuggles. He melts into me on the couch every night and *demands* I pet him the entire time. When I stop, he looks back at me with utter disgust and a pathetic look on his face. So, I keep petting him. It's like he's got me figured out or something.

Beau is the first dog I ever rescued, and what a life it has been since. I may have rescued him, but he also rescued me by giving my life a new purpose. He is nothing short of wonderful. He has inspired me to volunteer at animal rescues, foster animals, and adopt several more dogs in need along the way. Beau has been with me through so many things: two years of college, five different homes, four job changes, meeting the love of my life, getting married, buying my first house, and welcoming a human baby brother! He comforted me during my depression in college and buried me in snuggles when my dad passed away in 2015. Beau, put simply, makes things better. He is tolerant of every animal he meets, is patient, never has accidents in the house, and has a laid-back personality. But don't touch his paws while he's sleeping, he turns into a grumpy boy. Nobody's perfect, right?

Having seen the impact a loving home can make on a previously neglected animal, Beau inspired me to start fostering animals. I want others to see that impact as well. Rather than being overwhelmed and shut down in a rescue, an animal in a loving home feels more comfortable and safer, giving them the confidence to show their true personality. This should then help them get adopted quicker and reduce the chances of them being returned since their furever home will know more about them up front.

Being in a foster home can help identify "problems" with an animal sooner rather than later. For example, you can test if a dog is good with cats or other dogs in a rescue setting, but it may not speak to how they'll actually respond in a family home. They're likely stressed and may react poorly at the rescue. Whereas in a home, after they've had time to decompress, they may not be bothered by fellow pets. The transformation of these animals is amazing when they're in a home. It makes a substantial difference in their lives, and it can make a difference in your life, too.

I'm hoping to inspire and encourage other families to consider fostering animals. If you need some convincing, I'd like to help. You're about to meet and read about several incredible furry friends Stephanie and I have cared for in the following pages. Their journeys demonstrate how fostering an animal can change a life. But first, let me tell you a bit more about me, Emily – animal foster mom and advocate, real estate agent with Keller Williams Revolution in Bloomington, Illinois (shameless plug, and first of many), proud wife and mother.

"Once you have had a wonderful dog, a life without one, is a life diminished."

-Dean Koontz

The Rainbow Zoo

Shortly before I met Beau, my dog soulmate, I met my human soulmate and love of my life, Stephanie. We met at Illinois Wesleyan University in 2012 where we both attended college. A slight remix of a classic love story, the volleyball player meets the basketball player...and the rest is history. While her dry, sarcastic sense of humor drew me in, my goofy personality piqued her interest. Not to mention how beautiful she was! And, she still is beautiful, which I should probably mention before she catches that.

We started as friends and eventually began dating in May 2013. She is literally my "one and only." My first and last girlfriend, and now my wife. *What a ride we've been on!* We've grown up together and have formed a beautiful relationship and marriage. One of my favorite parts about our relationship is our shared love and passion for saving animals. I fostered a little bit in and after college, but our foster journey together really took off when we bought a home of our own in 2018.

If we've learned one thing from fostering animals, it's that any negative reactions, like a scared dog biting us or not getting along with our dogs right away, are likely due to their past trauma. It doesn't necessarily speak to the animals themselves. They just need time to decompress and learn to trust people. I cannot reiterate enough how important it is to give every animal the time and the chance to thrive and adjust to a healthy environment. I'll show you just how much time can change their lives as I talk about all of the animals that have been through our home.

Before I dive into our foster journey, I'd like to introduce our little family.

Stephanie is a school psychologist. She helps students in need of academic intervention and counseling. Outside of work, her love for Harry Potter is her main hobby. I'm convinced she thinks she's a witch (I originally called her a wizard, which *appalled* her, so it has now been corrected), but that's a story for another time. She also loves to read, binge watch her favorite Netflix shows, host game nights with our friends, and cook and bake.

Stephanie is the best dog, cat, and human mom. Speaking of, we are new moms to a beautiful baby boy, Louie, and are loving motherhood so far! I now understand why parents have a hard time describing just how much they love their children. It is a love like no other, and we are so blessed to get to experience life with him. As for me, as previously mentioned, I'm a real estate agent (if you're looking to buy, sell, or invest in real estate, I'm your girl) and I absolutely love my job. When I'm not helping people buy or sell homes, I love watching sports or Netflix, working out, walking our dogs, and spending time with my family and friends.

We have several dogs and a cat named Albus. Plus, a Russian tortoise named Freddy. All of the dogs have a chapter of their own, so you'll get to know them soon. Albus and Freddy do not have their own chapters (sorry, guys) so here is a bit more about them.

Stephanie brought Freddy home when she was eleven and he was just a wee tortoise. The average lifespan of a Russian tortoise is more than fifty years, but I'm convinced he may outlive us. In her younger days, not to throw her under the bus while also throwing her under the bus, Stephanie forgot to feed him quite a few times and he still survived (would not recommend this though). I think he would survive anything. For now, he is content in his big tank with his daily diet of carrots, spinach, and apples. I am also the one who always feeds him to avoid any more lapses in meals.

Now to introduce the real star of our house and the light of Stephanie's life, Albus. While in graduate school at Eastern Illinois University, Stephanie felt lonely. She lived by herself and needed a buddy, which came in the form of a cat. She could've just got a fish... Then again, when I was lonely, I adopted a dog, so I guess I shouldn't judge.

I did *not* take the news well when she told me about her plan to adopt Albus. Cats were not my jam, and I knew he'd likely live with me some day. It definitely caused an argument or two, but I eventually got over it and regretted how I handled it. After meeting Albus, he snuggled with me immediately. *Ew, but aw.* The little stinker turned me into a cat lover. I would describe Albus as an obnoxious meower, food inhaler, and nap king. He sleeps through most things and tolerates the chaos of all our dogs. In the rare event that he isn't fast asleep, he loves to play and chase strings around. Another cherished hobby of his is walking across my face and pillow at random hours of the night. *I* do not cherish this hobby. Stephanie would describe Albus as perfect with no flaws and potentially loves him more than she loves me.

Since our house resembles a zoo and we live on Rainbow Avenue, we refer to our home as "The Rainbow Zoo." People's eyes always widen when we mention how many pets we have. Despite all the animals residing within, it's not too overwhelming to live with them. Sure, when the dogs get to barking, it's like a howling symphony, but they calm down quickly and go back to napping. They also all get along with each other most of the time and entertain each other when they're playful. So how did we end up with so many animals? Two words: Foster Fortunes.

When we tell people we foster animals, we usually get a response that sounds something like, "Gosh I don't know how you do it, I wouldn't be able to." Or, "I wouldn't be able to give them up, I'd have ten dogs by now." Our response is either, "It gets easier with every animal," or, "Knowing they go to a good home makes it less painful." But the truth is, it doesn't get easier. And while knowing they find a good family does help, it still sucks every time. (Except for a few of them who were hell raisers at our house, *those* goodbyes were easier).

I'd love to tell you there's a secret to saying goodbye, but there's not and I don't want to sugar coat the raw emotions that come with fostering animals and letting them go. The hardest part is getting attached and then watching them drive away knowing there's a good chance we will never see them again.

I am certain becoming attached is one of the main reasons people don't foster. And I get that, but I would challenge you to try to focus on the impact you could have before the goodbye. You are saving and changing a life that may not have been saved without your help. How amazing is that? Plus, it will change your life, too. Not to mention it's a lot of fun! Meeting all sorts of different animals, spending time with them, chasing puppies through the yard, getting snuggles from a scared dog who finally trusts you, and so much more. Fostering is one of the greatest joys of my life.

For Stephanie and me, the pain and the goodbyes are always worth it because we know we played a part in their journey to find a happy life. Or, in a couple cases, were with them before they passed. The positive impact they have on our lives along the way cannot be explained in words. If you can maintain the mindset that you're saving a life, while accepting that it's going to be hard yet rewarding along the way, you can do great things for these animals, too.

Every rescue operates differently. We volunteer with Pet Central Helps (PCH) so our fostering experience typically starts like this:

The foster animals usually come to us in a similar condition; scared, not potty trained, curious as to what a toy is, unsure what love is, and have likely met more mean people than nice people.

We pick them up at the rescue, Pet Central Helps, after they receive any necessary vaccinations, nail trims, and an assessment. We put their crate, food, and other supplies in the trunk and either Stephanie or I will hold them on our way home. They almost always smell bad or have matted fur and an empty look in their eyes. We try to calm them down with soft voices, gentle pets, and tell them they're safe now.

For our foster dogs, the car ride is the calm before the storm. Pulling into the garage, we keep the leash or harness on and let them explore our fenced back yard. Then, one by one, we bring our dogs out so they can meet and have their butt sniffs. If needed, one of us sleeps in the guest room with the new arrival their first night so they can have space to themselves and relax without the other dogs around. The first night is almost always a sleepless night for us as we're constantly waking up to make sure the dog is comfortable and hasn't had any accidents.

For our foster cats, we bring them inside and put them in a separate room with no introductions to the other animals. Sometimes we will introduce them eventually and sometimes they are in the one room for their whole stay. They typically do just fine in the room by themself and we visit them frequently.

The foster animals just need a little time and space – they've already had a long day of transportation and new faces.

> Pro tip: there's a strong chance that dogs are going to have a potty-related accident in your house over the first few days. It's easier to prepare the cleaning supplies rather than obsess over stopping it from happening.

The days following include decompressing, getting to know them, lots of love and snuggles, and adjusting to a new environment. While the overall fostering process can be similar from animal to animal, I'd like to share with you the story of each and every animal who has joined us and what they taught us along the way.

Every rescue operates differently. Here are a few examples.

Pet Central Helps, located in Normal, Illinois, explains their operations:

Pet Central Helps is a 501(c)(3) no-kill animal rescue, helping McLean County and surrounding communities. They believe that financial circumstances alone are not reliable indicators of a potential successful adoption and strive to keep people and pets together. Pet Central Helps rescues cats and dogs of all ages, sizes, and breeds. They step in to take sick dogs surrendered to local vets, find and take in animals that need immediate care or have been hurt, as well as a balance of the highly adoptable ones to help with the medical costs. They house them in their physical shelter as well as in foster homes. There is no cost associated with fostering for them; they provide food, vet care, crates, toys, etc. The more families that foster, the more animals they can save. To apply to foster, you can fill out an application on their website which you can find on the reference page.

Andrea Williams, Director of Carolina Boxer Rescue explains their operations:

"Carolina Boxer Rescue is a 100% volunteer organization and is a foster-based rescue. We do not have a brick and mortar location. Our foster homes are scattered throughout NC, SC, VA, and the Northern parts of Georgia. The beauty of a foster-based rescue is, the dogs live in homes of the fosters and are treated as if they are one of the foster's own dogs.

When fostering - the foster provides the food for their dog, but vet appointments and medications are covered by the rescue. Some dogs in foster homes will require additional training before they can be adopted out, and the rescue also covers that.

Prior to becoming a foster, the applicant needs to put in an application and pass a vet reference check and 3 additional references. A home visit is then conducted to meet the applicant, view their home and then determine whether they will be a good foster or not.

Carolina Boxer Rescue is a breed-specific rescue, meaning we only take in boxers or boxer mix dogs. We pull from local area shelters and also take in owner-surrendered dogs. While each month varies with the number of dogs we take in, the rescue typically saves about 230 dogs per year. The rescue has been saving dogs since 2001 - that is a lot of saved dogs!"

Happy Tails

Meet Rex

I worked as a kennel help assistant at Wishbone Canine Rescue during the summer of 2014. I had taken the job about a year after adopting Beau due to my desire to help more dogs in need. I cleaned kennels, fed dogs, let them out to go potty, and so on. I really enjoyed it! I did not enjoy the difficulty of seeing all of the dogs looking for homes on a daily basis, but I saw plenty of them get adopted along the way which helped. I made it halfway through the summer when I met ten-month-old Rex. A little floof ball who had a "bite risk" label on his kennel and could not be adopted out to a family with young kids.

My heart pounded every time I had to let him out of his kennel. *Was he going to bite me?!* I remained patient with him and tried not to make any quick movements, but the stress levels were high. He never did try to bite me, but instead shook with fear. Always flinching and cowering when I put his leash on, something pulled me toward helping him more. After ten days of Rex's stay at the rescue, I made the impulsive decision to foster him. Emphasis on "impulsive." *My first foster dog! What do I do now? Would Beau even like him?* I will blame my impulsive, irresponsible decision making on my college-kid maturity level. I just felt so bad for Rex and wanted to get him out of there.

I packed up his stuff and brought him home without telling my room-mates; big mistake that I still regret today. Again... *college-kid* brain! Beau loved him and they got along great. I was able to breathe a sigh of relief. Retract said sigh of relief, because I soon discovered Remi did not like Rex, which made the whole fostering situation very difficult. I tried to just keep him in my room, but Remi went nuts at my door. I didn't want to take him back to the rescue, but it became clear we needed a new plan.

With this being my first foster dog, I hesitated to give up on him because I didn't want the rescue to think I was an unreliable foster. Plus, I worked there, and I didn't want them to think less of me. Did I mention I also have anxiety?

Determined to make it work for him, Stephanie and I came up with a decent plan. When I couldn't be at home with him, I took Rex to Stephanie's parents' house, where she lived during her gap year before graduate school. When home with my roommates, Beau, Rex, and I spent a good amount of time in my room to avoid added stress for Remi.

Once we figured out the logistics, Rex and I decompressed together. The little floof snuggled with me like a little sweetie pie. I watched him start to play and chase Beau around, and he looked like a completely different dog than when in his kennel. He still cowered at times, but it was clear he felt comfortable with us and trusted us by giving us kisses and not showing any signs of wanting to bite. I'm not sure how he gained his "bite risk" label as we saw no signs of that behavior. But he also wasn't in a kennel anymore which could have been the reason he used to try to bite. He seemed to be an excellent dog. I'm not saying the rescue mislabeled him; I just think his being in a home showed a completely different side to him. The beautiful thing about foster homes!

A friend of mine lived with us that summer, and her coworker had been looking for a small dog to adopt. Just one small catch: this coworker had two smaller kids. Remember, Rex is not supposed to go to a home with kids due to his "bite risk" label. However, I reached out to the rescue director and told her I think it would be worth trying a meet and greet to see how he does with kids. They were five and seven years old. I didn't sleep the night before the meet and greet because I just didn't know how it would go, but Rex was great and friendly with them!

About a week later they decided to make Rex a part of their family. The goodbye sucked and made me incredibly sad. I knew I couldn't keep him, nor did I have any intention of doing so, but I saw him completely morph into this new dog and then he just left forever. It was a very difficult thing for me to process. All of that time and effort and love just for him to leave. Despite grieving for a little while, my mentality began to shift. *How incredible that because of me he found his furever home?* I couldn't wait for the next opportunity to change a dog's life.

Meet Zeus

I would like to start this chapter with an apology to my roommate at the time, Sam, for thinking it was a good idea to foster a puppy. We lived together the year after I graduated college during Sam's senior year. I worked full time at Enterprise Rent-A-Car and Zeus woke up at the crack of dawn when I left, waking Sam up every morning with his whining. He did not like his crate at all. Not to mention the potty training and puppy energy in our house!

I no longer worked at Wishbone, but still volunteered there and took Zeus home one day. A prime example of my impulsive decision making yet again. *Note to self: make sure fostering a dog is okay with everyone you're living with. Unless it's your spouse...because, eh, they'll probably forgive you.* I'm kidding. Make sure it's okay! Back to Zeus; a beautiful brindle Mountain Cur mix pup.

More times than not, a rescue dog's breed is a best guess. Unless the rescue knows exactly what breed the mom and dad are. Sometimes it is very obvious what kind of dog they are, but other times it's a tossup. The rescues I've volunteered with do not do DNA tests either.

When the zooming around the house subsided, he liked to nap on our laps. Beau liked Zeus, too! *Did Beau need a permanent buddy?*

Perhaps. Not Zeus, though. I cherished my sleep and my friendship with Sam too much to make him a permanent resident.

After only a week of fostering, Zeus got an application from a girl about my age at the time (twenty-three) who had been considering getting a dog. She ended up adopting him but after a month or so, she decided the responsibility of having a puppy was too much for her at that time in her life. I stayed in close communication with her throughout that month and wished it would've worked out, but I also understood that she had to do what worked best for her. She returned Zeus and he went to another great foster home and then to a forever family. Someone came from Oklahoma to get him! #dedicated

My foster journey with Zeus taught me to always make sure my roommates are okay with a foster dog before bringing them home and to seriously consider before fostering a puppy next time. The energy is real, you will lose sleep, and you'll need a few bottles of all-purpose cleaner and carpet cleaner to make it through.

"We started fostering after having to put our four-teen-year-old dog down last year. We weren't ready to get another dog but hated the 'empty' house. We've now had nearly twenty fosters in a year and a half, somehow managing to only have one foster fail! It's been a wild ride of ups and downs, funny moments and loss, snuggles and bones. It's so amazing watching dogs go from being terrified of everything to living their best lives! And the best part is you get that 'we're getting a dog!' feeling every few weeks!"

-Kelly Reeves, foster for Pet Central Helps

Meet Bailey

I remember picking Bailey up at the rescue to foster her so vividly. She had been at the rescue the longest out of all the dogs there. At seven-years-old, she kept getting overlooked. The volunteers thought it might be because she was a black dog, in addition to her age.

The Spruce Pets reports that rescues all over the world have noticed that Black Dog Syndrome negatively effects adoption rates of black pets. The reason for this is unclear, but there are several theories as to why. One theory, explained by Cesar Millan, or The Dog Whisperer, is that people perceive black dogs to be more aggressive or evil. In movies and shows, black dogs are typically associated as aggressive and intimidating. Millan says Dobermans and Rottweilers, both dark in color, are often the attack dogs protecting the bad guys. Even if this representation doesn't affect a potential adopter, black dogs also have the disadvantage of their faces being difficult to see. This makes it harder to see their sad "adopt me" faces.

So, how do we fix this? One way is to simply give a black dog a chance. They are just as loving as any other dog, and Bailey is my proof of that.

When I let her out of her cage at the rescue, she sprinted towards the door and looked back at me with a toothy smile. She knew we were getting the heck out of there!

I took her home and introduced her to Beau. Instant besties. After some butt sniffing and living room zoomies, we took our first walk as a trio. Walking two dogs compared to one may not seem like much of a difference, but whoa. One smells something in one direction and the other's nose is pulling us the other way. I quickly realized I missed too many upper body workouts in the gym. After the adjustment period, we soon established a nice pace and agreement not to pull mom over into the street. Except when there are bunnies and squirrels nearby; the rules no longer apply when those pesky critters are close.

Our daily walks were the best part of our day, followed by lots of couch cuddles. Bailey fit in perfectly. But let's not forget she's my foster dog. As she adjusted to house life, she had a few accidents here and there. We also needed to work through her fear of being in a crate. She had a panic attack every time I put her in there, resulting in her tearing up her blankets and bed and biting at the metal crate wires. One time she made her mouth bleed, and I saw her teeth up close for the first time. Her top and bottom teeth in the front were almost chiseled down to the gums. She still had teeth, but they didn't look right.

I reached out to the volunteer team at the rescue, and they mentioned her intake paperwork noted someone found her in the basement of an abandoned house in a crate. When she came to the rescue, she had a large open wound down the middle of her head. I hate thinking about it, but I think she was desperately trying to escape being left behind. I don't know how many days she had been there by herself, but again, I'd rather not think about it, but this explained her crate anxiety.

When her head incision healed, it left her with a scar that generated a precious little mohawk on top of her head. I like to think of this as a representation of her life turning around for the better.

I checked in with the rescue volunteers every few days to see if she had any adoption applications. She never did, which got me thinking. Does she belong with us? Are two dogs better than one? (The answer is always "yes," by the way). After about a month of fostering, I decided I just couldn't let her go.

Bailey chose me as her person from the very start. I think it must be because she finally felt safe when she came home with me. She still follows me everywhere around the house and loves to sleep next to me at night.

Due to her previous trauma and abuse, she has her quirks. She can be selective with dogs who make her nervous, and there is something about children that throws her into a defensive panic if they approach her without warning. Maybe children were not kind to her in the past, or it could just be because kids can be unpredictable. We will never really know, but there's an obvious shift in her personality when they're around. We just keep her away from them to make sure everyone stays safe.

Bailey is fourteen-years-old now and is my fearless companion. With age has come more neediness, but I don't mind. Our old girl needs help getting on and off the bed and is losing her hearing a little bit. Especially if she's in a deep sleep! I envy her ability to sleep through just about anything. Hearing seems to be most difficult for her when she's outside and I'm calling her to come inside...I think that may just be selective hearing.

She still loves her long walks and chasing squirrels in the back yard. There is certainly some pep left in her step. It's been a mix of emotions to watch her age, and I dread her final day with us, but she is just another example of giving dogs a chance.

Bailey's apparent "flaw" of not liking kids concerned us when Stephanie became pregnant. We knew it was inevitable though because we've always wanted children of our own. Once Louie arrived, we brought him home from the hospital to meet our squad. All of the dogs did great with him, to our relief! Beau seems to be the most interested in him, and Bailey hasn't shown any signs of aggression. She sniffs him here and there but mainly keeps her distance.

She sometimes lays near him while he's on his play mat and just watches him. Could it be because she wants his stuffed animals? Absolutely. We shall see what she does when Louie becomes "grabby" and mobile, but for now we are confident she won't cause him any harm and plan to always keep a close eye/not take any chances. We have baby gates and are prepared to maintain a distance between them should any future issues arise. Once we get all of our dogs under control with him, we are both looking forward to sharing our passion of fostering animals with Louie throughout his life.

If a dog is in the rescue for a long time, people naturally tend to think there's something wrong with them. If there wasn't, they'd be adopted by now, right? (This theory holds true in the housing market too if a house is on the market for a while. Sorry, my Realtor brain can't help itself.) Except price and condition aren't typically a problem when it comes to adoptable dogs as it is with houses for sale.

Don't overlook the dogs that have been there for a long time simply due to the length of their stay. Ask questions, get to know them; you might be surprised there is nothing wrong with them. They just haven't met the right family yet. Sure, some dogs might need to be the only animal in the home or go to no children homes, so they are likely going to take more time to find a home, but there are plenty of families out there who just want one dog or have no kids.

Meet Theo

A picture of Theo, a then six-year-old chihuahua with the cutest face, big ol' ears, and wide, buggy eyes made its way onto my Facebook feed from our foster parents Facebook group. (If you're thinking *"wow that sounds adorable, I wish I could see what he looked like."* Fear not. All of our foster animals' photos are on my website.)

Before I could show Stephanie or comment on the post, another foster family scooped him up, and he got adopted even quicker. A few weeks later, I arrived at our weekly Saturday adoption event, and I saw someone holding Theo.

"Didn't this dog get adopted?" I asked.

"His owner brought him back just this morning because he had too many accidents in the house," the volunteer replied.

I come to find out these owners left him home alone for eighteen hours or longer at a time... Um, I would pee on the floor, too. A dog shouldn't be expected to hold their bladder for that long, ever. The volunteer asked me to hold him, and then it was game over. Before I knew it, he came home with me as our new foster dog. Don't worry, Stephanie approved. Another family had met him at the same event and decided to adopt him the next weekend. We agreed to foster him for a week.

He got along well with Bailey and Beau at first, as long as they respected his space. Little chihuahuas are usually the bossiest and sassiest. Theo was no exception! Stephanie and I thought about adopting him, but as I lived in an apartment with a roommate and two dogs, I didn't think it could work. Then Stephanie asked if we could adopt Theo if he got brought back again. Confidently thinking he found his furever home with his next adopters, I agreed. Well, what do you know, the little shit got returned *again*! This adopter brought him back because he didn't play enough with their other dog. Theo is absolutely a couch potato, so this didn't surprise us.

We *had* to keep him! He had been given up twice now, and we didn't want him to go through it again. Plus, I already told Stephanie we could, and she does not let things like that go. I once made the mistake of telling her we could get ice cream, then changed my mind...long story short, we still got ice cream.

We don't know much about Theo's history, but suspect he has been through some trauma due to what we do know. One of his ears is missing a little off the top and he has a few scars on his back, plus he nervously pees and cowers if you raise your voice or go to pet the top of his head. We learned this is called submissive urination, when a dog pees as a response to anxiety or fear. Puppies who are still gaining confidence can experience this behavior, but it can also occur in adult dogs with a history of trauma. Some dogs also just pee out of pure excitement which is a little different. Submissive urination can be triggered by a loud noise like a firework or siren, a person approaching a dog too quickly, or someone yelling at the dog.

Theo requires a good amount of patience, as he still has accidents in the house (we put a belly band, which is a male doggy diaper, on him when we leave the house for extended periods of time). He has successfully scooted out of this belly band numerous times, if he's feeling up for that kind of effort. I've watched him on our doggy camera use the kitchen chair to remove it...at least it's entertaining.

Speaking of pee...if it's raining, good luck getting him outside to go potty. I've lost track of the number of times I've had to pick up the twelve-pound potato and place him in the yard to go to the bathroom. Even after dropping him by his favorite pee tree, he usually stares at me cowering and squinting through the rain drops for a few minutes before agreeing to do his business. Sometimes it's not worth the battle, and I just put a diaper on him until the rain subsides.

His primary habitat is buried under a blanket on the couch, but he does like to take walks every now and then. Not on a hot day though. He will lay in the grass and stare at us, refusing to move, if we make him walk when it's above seventy-five degrees. We've had to carry him home on several occasions.

His signature trait is his breath. This stench has earned him the nickname of "dumpster goblin" because his mouth literally smells like the inside of a dumpster. And he kind of looks like a goblin with his goofy little smile (he's missing several front teeth) and beady eyes. We've gotten his teeth professionally cleaned three times and give him daily dental treats, and he still makes us gag if he gets too close. If we ever lost him in the neighborhood, I'm certain the smelly trail of his breath would lead us to him.

Despite his toxic mouth, we love him more than anything. He rules the house and makes sure the other dogs know who is boss! Glimpses of fear and past trauma are still present, but he is thriving as a member of our family. He has also become my real estate assistant. I feature him in my marketing and a picture of his face lives on the back window of my car next to a punny saying about real estate and dogs. The fame hasn't gotten to him yet and he hasn't requested any payment for his services. Free food and housing seems like an even trade to me.

"Not only has fostering done so much for animals we have brought into our home but it has been an amazing experience for my children. They have learned to love and let go. They have learned the importance of giving as much love as they can in the short time we have them and they too have seen the impact love can have after just a few days or weeks and watch the transformation. My hope for them is that they learn that all animals are worth saving and being loved!"

-Cassandra Ann, foster for Pet Central Helps

Meet the Beauty and the Beast Puppies

Stephanie and I closed on our first house in June of 2018. Naturally, we wanted to foster a litter of puppies once we had more space and no landlord rules. And not just little puppies...big black lab mix puppies. We were in *way* over our heads to say the least. Firstly, our dogs don't really like puppies because the little energy balls don't understand boundaries. Secondly, we didn't have a carpet-free room for the puppies to stay in, so they took over our living room (puppy accidents are frequent, do not put them in a carpeted room). We had laminate floors in the living room that ended up becoming slightly warped due to the puppy pee and water spills. And lastly, *there were five of them!* Lesson learned... becoming a homeowner does not mean you're ready to foster five large puppies.

I have relayed this realization to my first-time homebuyers, too. Despite the headache, they were adorable, and it seemed to be worth it (I think). On top of the messiness, they all got worms and needed medicine every day.

Disclaimer: If you're a spaghetti lover or nearing mealtime, it could take a few days, weeks, or months to recover after reading this. The worms resulted in what looked like spaghetti in their poop. What a joy it was picking that up! (The worms cleared up quickly though. Worms are common with puppies so don't be alarmed and notify the rescue vet if you notice them.)

Have I convinced you to foster puppies yet? I actually do not write this to discourage you from fostering puppies; I just want to make sure you have a plan and know what could lie ahead. It can be extremely fun and entertaining if you have the patience and the house set up for it. Key items: Puppy pen, puppy pads, paper towels, and multipurpose cleaner.

Belle, Gaston, Mrs. Potts, Enchantress, and LeFou loved to play outside.

They also loved to eat things, anything really. Our heads were always on a swivel to make sure they weren't eating non-edible items. I imagine our neighbors viewed some great entertainment witnessing us run from fence to fence keeping an eye on all five of them. Needless to say, we didn't relax most of the time they were awake.

We only let them around our dogs when all dogs were outside to allow for enough room for our grumpy dogs to escape them.

If the puppies released enough energy, they slept great all night (about ten p.m.-seven a.m.). I remember laying in their puppy pen with them at night to get them to calm down and go to sleep. They were sweet and grew quickly. At their first adoption event, not one of them got adopted. We were surprised since puppies are usually very sought after. Plus, they were lab mixes, and many adopters look for that breed. We loved them, but we were ready for a break from the puppy energy and poop palooza. Sometimes we are more than ready to say goodbye to our foster animals.

They became too much for us so another foster family took them after their week-long stay at our house. She had more room for them to run; they had quickly grown from cute and little to taking over our entire house. Eventually, all of the little spaghetti poop monsters found their furever homes.

We haven't fostered many litters of puppies since then... but we've never regretted fostering any animal. Some are just tougher than others, which makes us appreciate the easy ones even more. If you have the setup, fostering puppies is very fun! We have several foster families who love to foster litters of them. I imagine it's kind of like being an aunt, uncle, or grandparent and being able to give the baby back to mom and dad eventually.

Meet Balto

Balto looked exactly like the famous dog sled hero straight out of the Disney movie. A playful pup, but not too crazy for our temporary household. Did we watch the movie *Balto* with him? Yes. And he actually seemed to watch it! He warmed up to us from the start, loved his squeaky toys, and had very few accidents in the house.

We were sure to let him out frequently to avoid said accidents, but avoiding them completely is unrealistic given his age and recent arrival to a new environment. Our dogs didn't love him, but they didn't hate him either. Maybe they were jealous of his sled dog fame? But more likely it's because his energy didn't always match theirs. While we did not experience any issues between the dogs, we kept a close eye to make sure they didn't get into any disagreements.

His *huge* ears stood straight up most of the time. They literally flopped in the wind as he ran around the back yard. I still regret not getting a slow-motion video. We could've gone viral. Not to mention his body hadn't yet caught up to the size of those ears. Pretty cute!

He stayed with us for a few days, because c'mon, he's practically famous and absolutely adorable. We anticipated his stay to be short due to his age and cuteness, but we never really know how long a dog will be with us. They could come down with a cough (which places them on medical hold and doesn't allow them to be adopted until they're better), or not get applications right away, etc. We appreciate every moment. I love the short puppy stays because it makes it easier to say goodbye when we haven't had a ton of time to get attached. Also, puppies are always cuter when you don't have to train them much.

An active family with small kids and dogs adopted Balto. I haven't seen any updates about him over the years, but I'm confident he is in good hands. No news is usually good news!

"In 2018, my family went to a local pet store to pick up a few items for my husband's fish tank. It was during that time Pet Central Helps was holding an adoption event. We fell in love with ALL THE DOGS. At the event, a woman named Stephanie introduced us to the idea of "Pet Fostering" which was a completely new concept to us. My kids, of course, were super excited.

We filled out all necessary paperwork and were approved to foster! Over the course of the next few years, my family fostered about thirty-five dogs. We can tell you stories about each one. We didn't realize the impact we would be having on these scared, innocent souls. Each of them needed a stable, loving environment to learn, heal and grow. My family was a steppingstone to begin a new, healthy life. By fostering in a home environment, it frees up space in rescues and gives each animal the one on one attention it deserves.

Some foster dogs only needed short term care until they were ready to be adopted and others needed months. While it was sad to see them go, we were so happy for them as they were adopted into loving families. To remember each dog that we fostered, we stamped their paw print in paint on a framed poster board and hung it in our hallway. We proudly display a painting full of different shapes and sizes of paws that have each touched our hearts in so many ways."

-Laura Claver, foster for Pet Central Helps

Meet Moana

"Make way, make way...for Moana," a medium-sized mama pup, who crashed with us for the weekend while her permanent foster went on a short trip. Fostering is a team effort! You're not alone in it. If you need backup because you're going on vacation or need to go out of town, reach out to other fosters to see if they can help out. We were the backup family for Moana.

Her puppies had been adopted (thank goodness they weren't at our house) so it was just her as our temporary house guest. What a good girl she turned out to be! She slept most of the time, likely recovering from raising her puppies and finally getting time to herself. We didn't have any problems with her and our dogs despite her being as big as Bailey and Beau. As they've aged, they sometimes get intimidated by large dogs, but Moana did just fine with them.

Theo didn't care either; as long as his slumber and spot on the couch aren't disturbed, he is unphased. Unless the mailman dares to drop our mail off, at which point Theo awakens and "protects" the house for us. We thoroughly enjoyed our weekend with Moana and fell in love with her after just forty-eight hours. Plus, she seemed to be potty trained which we *love*. What a great dog!

Signing up for a temporary foster over a weekend is a great idea if the unknown amount of time intimidates you. These short stays are typically very manageable and less stressful since you know exactly when they're being picked up.

Meet Lonnie

Lonnie, also known as Lon Bon Von Trap per Stephanie's nickname for him, had a calm personality, did well with our animals, and loved to go for long walks. He got a bit nervous with new people but became friends with them after a few minutes. Trying to get him to eat required patience and creativity; talk about picky! We mixed dry food with wet food, dry food with chicken stock, and a series of other combinations. Combo #5 ended up doing the trick: dry food, wet food, shredded chicken, and chicken stock.

> Pro tip: It is common for foster animals, especially dogs, to be picky with food for a couple of days (unless they are severely malnourished). Be patient with them and try a few different combinations. Chicken broth over the food has been a consistent winner for us. They'll eat eventually once they get hungry enough too. If their lack of appetite persists and they're acting lethargic, consult with the rescue's vet to be sure there are no medical concerns.

We cooked a more gourmet meal for him than for ourselves some nights. We also had to trick him and sneak a Benadryl in the meal to help him recover from his sneezing and allergies. Some dogs are stubborn when it comes to pill taking. A journey indeed, but we figured it out. Lonnie enjoyed being in his crate, which can be rare with foster dogs, and would sleep in it all through the night. He even enjoyed spending time in it with the door open as he relaxed and took naps throughout the day.

He chose Stephanie as his person from the start and they became attached to each other. While fostering him, we had a weekend wedding and asked another foster, Bridget, to watch him. Bridget is an awesome foster, so we knew he'd be in good hands, but Stephanie struggled and cried as we said goodbye.

The thought of never seeing him again and not being there for him on his potential adoption day visibly upset her. We strongly prefer to attend our foster dogs' adoption events to answer questions potential adopters have and meet the families ourselves. It gives us peace of mind when we get to meet the adopters. Luckily for her, he did not get adopted and we picked him up when we were back in town.

The following weekend, a single woman adopted Lonnie, and she seemed to be a great fit for him. She had him for a few weeks but then emailed us stating that Lonnie had bitten her dad on the hand despite meeting him a few times prior to that day. Lonnie also lunged at his adopter with teeth bared which ultimately made her too nervous to keep him around. We tried to connect her with our rescue behavior team, who offer free advice and training, but Lonnie bit someone at training class, too.

This behavior confused us; we hadn't seen any signs of aggression from him before this. We were perplexed and concerned, and tried to figure out where this behavior came from. We agreed to take him back and noticed immediately that he appeared to be a very different dog. We're not sure what happened, but he began getting aggressive toward our cat (who he never cared about before).

His attachment to Stephanie also grew much stronger. This attachment caused him to become snarly towards me, as if I were a threat to Stephanie. First, he would growl at me here and there but then he would attempt to bite me if I got too close or tried to put him in his crate. This aggression stressed both of us out. Stephanie had to come home from work one day to help me put him in his crate so I could go back to my workplace after my lunch break. Lonnie stood on the top of the couch and would lunge at me if I got too close. We were able to manage this behavior for a while, until it became too much.

On our last night with him, I let the dogs outside to go potty and yelled at Beau

for nearly tripping me. Lonnie lost it. He didn't go after anyone or anything in particular, but he started barking and growling loudly, almost like he switched into "Kujo" mode. I opened the door to go inside, and he ran right into his crate. I had gotten the door to his crate closed but not latched and called Stephanie to come help me. Lonnie bit her finger. We had hit our breaking point. Stephanie cried and cried and feared he would no longer be able to be in our home. *If he reacted like this to Stephanie, who he adored, what was going on?* We couldn't get him under control. We took him in for an evaluation by our animal behavior specialist. She tried some things with him to determine what might be causing the aggressive behavior, what his fear triggers might be, and what worked to help calm him down. Some of his behavior seemed to come from resource guarding Stephanie, some from fear of men, and other fears we couldn't identify. We determined it would be best to put him in a new environment outside of our home to give him his best chance at thriving.

His best environment needed to be in a single woman home with structure. He needed to find someone who would not allow him to be the alpha in the home and who had more training experience to work with him. We loved him so incredibly much and having to move him some- where else broke our hearts, especially Stephanie's. We called Bridget for help, and she offered to take him without any hesitation. Bridget's home offered a very calm environment with more senior dogs; plus, she didn't live with anyone else. She had incredible fostering experience and a lot of training knowledge. She was perfect for him and so kind and reassuring as she knew we were struggling with this decision. We wanted what was best for Lonnie, and she was it.

Stephanie carried guilt for a long time about having to give him to someone else. I certainly struggled with this too, but she had become so close to him. She felt like she had failed Lonnie and beat herself up for not being able to fix him. We are both naturally empathetic people and want to help. Unfortunately, our home is not the best fit for every animal. We knew we gave him our best effort and made the right call. After a long time trying to get him adopted, Bridget ended up adopting him. Lonnie certainly had his flaws, but she built a wonderful environment for him where he could thrive.

This difficult experience and decision showed us how valuable our foster group is. Everyone is there to help, offer advice, and step in to take an animal if it makes sense for their home. These are people who share our passion for saving animals and are going through similar things. Take advantage of this support and connection! It can be a game changer.

"Why do I foster? Fostering animals is working towards saving lives and helping animals towards a safe and loving home. Is it hard to let them go? Yes. Is it incredibly hard work at times? Yes, not all fosters are easy but we take the time to work with them and build them into trusting companions for their family. Do I fall in love with them and cry when they leave? Yes. But, does that keep me from doing it? No. It's harder for me to know they are living a life of abuse, neglect, starvation or lack of human interaction than the sadness I feel when they get adopted and leave my arms.

Eventually the sadness fades as you see them living their best life with their new family and see how they finally feel safe and have molded into their love. Fostering animals has taught me so much about the love and forgiveness animals have; that which many humans seem to lack. It can be hard work at times but it is rewarding knowing the lives you have helped to save."

-Erin Sluis, foster for Pet Central Helps

Meet Captain Jack

Do you know those Swiffer dusters, the heavy-duty brand? That's what fluffy little Captain Jack resembled. I did not attempt to use him to dust our floors...but I'm certain they'd be sparkling and dust free if I did. Captain Jack, a crazy little puppy weighing maybe two pounds, arrived at the rescue all by himself, which is unusual. Usually, puppies arrive with at least one sibling. We still aren't sure of his previous situation.

Upon bringing the Swiffer duster home, our dogs were not a fan of him and his energizer bunny personality. Our dogs need their space and since puppies don't know what boundaries are, it ends up being stressful for us and them. But if it's only for a short period of time, it's manageable! Plus, Captain Jack's size and inability to jump on the couch meant he couldn't get to our grumpy dogs if they were up on the couches. He did try though. His little legs bounced up and down as he whined to get up on the couch. Eventually he gave up and would lay in his blanket kingdom nearby that we built for him.

My favorite foster dog video to date is the one I have of Captain Jack discovering his reflection in our oven door. He went nuts barking and howling at it; he would not be defeated by this seemingly threatening little floofy reflection. This duel became his favorite activity as he revisited the oven door often.

When not challenging his reflection, he tried to torment our dogs or laid on our laps. He ran at either one hundred percent or two percent. We enjoyed the two percent more. We only had Captain Jack for a few days before another foster parent, who had interest in adopting him, took over. A few days were plenty–our dogs were getting impatient, and we were getting overwhelmed with keeping everyone happy. This new foster parent ended up adopting him, too! Since we were friends with her, we are able to see pictures of him as he grew up. Captain Jack's growth resulted in reduced fluffiness, making him look more like a standard Swiffer duster rather than a heavy duty one.

Meet Boone

We met Boone, a small, ten-pound Jack Russell mix, at a fall adoption event. Our rescue director had him at her house, but felt he needed a foster home that had someone who could spend more time with him. The JRT breed made us a little anxious as they are known to be hyper. As you've read, we don't do well with hyper in our household. But as he sat on my lap throughout the event, so content and well-behaved, he suckered me into asking Stephanie if we could foster him. Stephanie and I decided to give him a try.

It seemed as though Boone walked into our house and thought to himself, "How quickly can I pee on everything in here?" He loved to mark his territory. Boone's marking may have been triggered by the urine smell of other dogs (thanks Theo) or because he didn't understand that peeing indoors isn't appropriate. Or both!

> Pro tip: Make sure you have belly bands, which are doggy diapers that wrap around the pelvis area, for your male foster dogs. The rescue may have some you can borrow. If they don't, they're worth the purchase and can be found on Amazon.

Ninety percent of our male foster dogs mark immediately when they get to our house, so we did expect some of it. Boone's marking gave us a run for our money though. Good thing our couches were hand-me-downs.

We used the belly bands 24/7 for him when inside. If you're considering fostering, just know this behavior is common and can be corrected.

An article by VCA Animal Hospitals, "Dog Behavior Problems Marking Behavior," discusses how normal marking is, especially for male dogs when they're in a new location with new smells and new people. They go on to mention how marking is one way dogs communicate and claim their territory. Belly bands can significantly help reduce your frustration as the dog gets used to all of the newness of the territory.

The belly bands are not a permanent fix, they are instead just a tool you can use as you're potty training them. If you don't want to work much on potty training that's also fine; you can use belly bands while the dogs are inside your house.

We were hopeful that after Boone got neutered his marking would decrease, which we noticed happened in the past with other male foster dogs after neutering. Boone's marking only decreased a little bit after being neutered and he still had a long way to go. In all honesty, we do not like nor try hard to potty train our foster dogs. We do the best we can, but it's difficult to commit, knowing they'll be with us for only a short time. And we might be kind of lazy about it, too.

Boone went to a "foster to adopt" home for almost a week, but his desire to urine mark everywhere deterred them from making it permanent. A foster to adopt home is where a family agrees to foster the animal for a maximum of one week to see if the animal will fit well into their household. If it doesn't work out, they can return the dog within seven days. I'm not sure how common this program is for other rescues; if it is something you're interested in, I would reach out to your local rescue directly to check.

Boone's return made us step up our potty-training game in the hopes he would be better for his next family. We didn't want this to be a recurring problem for potential adopters. Slowly but surely, his desire to pee everywhere decreased; we were winning the exhausting battle one less drop of pee at a time. Boone got adopted by a fantastic woman who planned to travel and take him on loads of adventures! When his tinkle tantrums did not intimidate her, we knew they were a perfect match.

Since Theo has a marking problem, it's no surprise when foster dogs walk in and want to mark over his urine. We clean our couches and protect them with blankets to try and prevent this. Boone's marking desire was our most severe marking problem to date. It tested our patience but we learned a lot. Be prepared to reduce your frustration. Get belly bands, keep a close eye, correct them when they have accidents, limit them to certain areas of the house, etc. It can certainly be frustrating, but we try not to take it out on them. They likely have no idea what they're doing is wrong as they haven't been taught what is proper. And some dogs, like Theo, are just a**holes and require extra patience and Lysol.

"I love fostering to open cages for more dogs to find a forever home. I love being able to socialize the puppies and teach them human hands are meant to show love. It is so fun to watch a scared dog gain confidence and see a twinkle in their eye when they feel safe. I love the part when they get adopted and the adopters reach out to me with progress, family pics with the pups, and how much joy they have brought into their lives."

-Candace Swenson, former foster for Pet Central Helps

Meet Drake

A good Samaritan found Drake running along the side of the highway with five other dogs. It looked like they had been dumped, since there were so many of them it's unlikely they had randomly escaped. Volunteers were able to catch most of them and get them to the rescue. The rescue who captured them was already overflowing and needed backup, so our rescue stepped in.

I remember seeing Drake's picture in our Foster Parents Group on Facebook. He looked miserable with bright red, irritated skin and minimal fur throughout his body. His ribs were prominent as well. Poor guy needed food and medication ASAP.

A look of defeat covered his skinny little face. We weren't supposed to get him as a foster since we had already signed up for another dog, Suzie, this time around. However, rearrangements were made; he ended up in the back of our car and then at our house. Driving home with both Suzie and Drake in our car made my mind race and my blood pressure rise. *One foster dog overwhelmed us enough, and now we have two?!* Plus, Drake's condition made me nervous. I had no idea what we were getting ourselves into. I tried to talk myself down and focus on the fact they both needed us. The stressful situation resolved itself quickly when another foster family took Suzie the next morning. Now we just had Drake. Way more manageable!

Drake clung to Stephanie right away. It's common for previously abused dogs to cling to one person when they finally feel safe, just like Bailey did with me. Drake didn't necessarily dislike me, but I did get quite a bit of side eye from him. He had a slew of medications from the vet, with the most important one being medicated shampoo to get his skin infection under control. He had little desire to do much of anything...besides cuddle with Stephanie of course. I cannot imagine how uncomfortable he must've been.

We gave him medicated baths every few days, and slowly but surely the redness dissipated. Every day he seemed happier and more comfortable. We also fattened him up as best as we could. He ate his food at an incredible speed! I would too if I had been starved most of my life. We did end up getting him a food bowl that made him eat slower. These are called slow feeder dog bowls and you can find them online or in stores. Some dogs eat too fast, and it makes them puke. Even if they don't puke, it's easier on their bellies if they eat at a slower pace. These bowls are a great option to help with that.

At the time we fostered Drake, our dogs Bailey, Beau, and Theo were permanent residents at the Rainbow Zoo (plus Albus, I feel like I forget to mention him because he spends most of his time snoozing). They welcomed him with almost open arms. Theo can be picky to put it lightly, but he got over it eventually. We watched Drake zoom around the back yard and finally start to enjoy the dog life. That's our favorite part to watch; a neglected and sad dog becoming comfortable and happy.

We took him to his first adoption event, and he went to a foster to adopt home.

Unfortunately, Drake got brought back because he tried to hunt their cats. We hadn't (yet) seen this behavior with Drake and Albus, but Albus isn't highly active and maybe the other cats were. We fostered him for another week and then off to the next event we went. We dropped him off at the adoption event but couldn't stay because we had plans in Chicago.

I remember one of the volunteers calling us saying he had gone to another foster to adopt home, and I bawled my eyes out. *He didn't even really like me, why did this make me so upset?!* I didn't get to say a proper goodbye, and it broke my heart thinking about never seeing him again. A few days later though he got brought back again due to him trying to attack another cat.

The following weekend the rescue had adoption events on both Saturday and Sunday. Two different families were interested in Drake and said they'd be back Sunday with a final decision, which made our stomachs turn. *Is he supposed to stay with us? What if he and Albus eventually didn't get along?* About ten minutes before the adoption event began on Sunday, we decided we couldn't let him go. We quickly called the adoption team to let them know we'd be keeping him for good.

Turns out he definitely does not like cats. After we adopted him he started going after Albus. He goes after squirrels and bunnies in a similar fashion so we think it's just a hunting instinct of his. We have given him several talks and PowerPoint presentations showing that Albus is a cat, not a squirrel or bunny. With redirection and a close watch, his behavior and desire to hunt Albus is manageable. We make sure Albus has space up high where he can escape and relax without Drake's wrath upon him. We also have baby gates and separate them at times of the day so Albus can have free reign without his head being on a swivel.

Drake is living his best life! He loves to hunt in the back yard for critters, go for walks, chew on his bones, play with his furry siblings, and chase tennis balls.

Sometimes I look back at the photos of when he first got to our house and while they always make me sad, it's incredible to see how much he has changed. All he needed was some love, medicated shampoo, and a warm, safe home with people he trusts.

If you see a dog that needs medical attention, try not to let it intimidate you. I'll admit, when I saw Drake's picture, his condition deterred me a bit from wanting to take him. *How long would it take to heal? Would he be with us for weeks, or months?* Joke's on me, he never left. But in all seriousness, I am so glad we took him in. Watching him heal and visibly show signs of relief over time has inspired us to help animals like him regardless of their health condition. The rescue provided us with the medication he needed, too. We are thrilled Drake found his way to us. He still prefers Stephanie's company to mine, but he does love me, too (usually when Stephanie isn't around though, #flattering).

Meet Glenda

The *cutest* little face peered at me through its metal crate while I was volunteering at an adoption event. Glenda, owner of said cutest face, came to the rescue with a group of six teeny tiny chihuahuas. Did we go to the event with the intention of bringing home a foster dog? Nope. But that's just how life goes sometimes. We scooped her right up and away we went. Glenda, a one-year-old chihuahua mix, weighed just four pounds. Told you she was teeny tiny. She could've used a little more meat on her bones, but her tiny body suited her. Just a petite purse puppy.

We fostered her in the winter, so we put a little pink sweater on her to keep her warm. A tiny baby peanut in a little sweater? Yes, you are correct, it was adorable. She took up hardly any space which is always appreciated in a small house full of several animals. Glenda came to us a little timid, but she warmed up to both us and our dogs quickly. It concerned me that Bailey and Drake might mistake her for a squirrel to hunt, but we had no issues there.

She loved both of us, but Glenda attached to my hip from day one and never left. She followed me *everywhere*. She could even be classified as my emotional support bathroom buddy. I also thought she might have a built-in pogo stick since she could jump into my arms from the floor with little to no effort. Our favorite game! The fosters that get attached to me make me dread adoption day even more because I get extra attached to them, too.

Glenda ventured out to greet others occasionally, but she mostly stayed close to me. We considered keeping her, as we do with most small dogs because we love them so much, but our voice of reason is usually stronger than our desire to keep them. Plus, we had recently adopted

Drake so the inn was full.

One of our fellow fosters reached out and said she had the perfect adopter for miss Glenda. She knew of a younger boy who recently lost his dog and needed a snuggle buddy to fill the void and repair his broken heart. Glenda would be perfect for him. When he and his dad showed up at the adoption event, the boy started crying happy tears. Glenda warmed up to him right away and cuddled up in his arms. My eyes filled with happy and sad tears. His and her happiness radiated, causing the happy tears, but the void I felt without my little buddy gave me a lump in my throat and the sad tears.

It's always an adjustment coming home without our fosters around anymore, but this one turned out to be an extra difficult adjustment for me. I didn't need to watch my step anymore in fear of squishing her or peek over my shoulder looking for her. A weird and sad feeling, but we knew how much her new best friend needed her, which brought us more joy than sadness.

"Oftentimes when I first pick up a foster dog they're frightened and unsure of what is going on. A mere shell of themselves. However, after a few days you can see them transform and blossom. They become more secure and confident and relaxed. Most times they even start to look better. Putting on weight, coats get shinier, eyes sparkle. Watching these changes is SO rewarding. It's only part of the reason I foster. I believe every animal deserves a chance at life and a loving forever home."

-Stacy Zook, foster for Pet Central Helps and Deeby's Senior Chihuahua Rescue

Meet Gunner

Gunner had been adopted from Pet Central Helps as a puppy. One day, PCH received a call that a dog of theirs had been surrendered to the Peoria Animal Control. All PCH animals are microchipped so if they get lost or returned somewhere other than the rescue, we are notified. A volunteer picked up Gunner, now more than sixty pounds, and brought him back to the rescue. She said he looked completely shut down; a sad face, not responding to food or pets, and seemingly a broken spirit. We don't have any idea what his life looked like before that day, but I can't imagine it was good. It's better that we don't know.

Gunner went to a great foster home for a couple of days, but the foster could not get him to come out of his crate after three whole days. She also had young children and felt her house may be a little too chaotic for him, which could have stunted his progress. She felt it would be best for him to go to a new foster home. Stephanie and I saw her post in the foster parents' group and decided we wanted to give him a chance to come out of his shell at our house.

We borrowed a wire "X pen" from a fellow foster (thanks, Jenn), which is just a large pet pen with a top (kind of like a lid). We wanted him to feel safe and have plenty of space. We also put a gate up in the doorway of his room so our dogs couldn't bother him. We kept this door open so he could at least look around our house and so our dogs could see him. When our dogs can't see what's going on inside a room, they whine and sniff like crazy, so it's always best to avoid that for the sake of our sanity.

I purposely pet one of our dogs right outside the gate, and Gunner stared at me with curious eyes and ears. I am convinced seeing our dogs and how I interacted with them boosted his confidence. I hoped it would help him understand that we were nice and weren't going to hurt him. It worked! Gunner wanted out of the X pen after only an hour at our house. This was amazing progress seeing as he hadn't come out after three days at the previous foster home. We let him out to wander around the room. He came right up to the gate to sniff our dogs. He then sat on our laps (despite being significantly larger than a typical lap dog) and gave us kisses. I went to sit in the living room, and I heard him whining. He wanted to come and hang out with us. Happy tears! He felt safe.

Our two bigger dogs, Beau and Bailey, who I mentioned before don't always like dogs bigger than them, did okay with him. We remained cautious when they were near each other. Overall, everyone did great! Once out of the X pen, Gunner transformed into a new dog. Loud noises and sudden movements still spooked him, and he didn't like men that much (likely due to past trauma). Good thing we have no men in our household ;). He met a few of our male friends and became very submissive, but he made progress quickly. Unfortunately, Bailey started to not be so fond of him causing food guarding with negative reactions, so we decided it would be best for Gunner to go to another foster home.

We try to avoid moving dogs around from home to home so they don't have to continually readjust, but sometimes it just doesn't work out. He went to another awesome foster home and continued to thrive! Gunner got adopted by an incredible family who accepted the fact he needed time, and they continued to work with him to boost his confidence. He remained nervous around new people, so his family brought him to the rescue's free training classes to help with socialization. Stephanie went into the class one day to visit him, and he immediately started licking her face when she sat down next to him. His tail whipped back and forth with excitement. The two trainers were shocked to see him act so friendly and social. He hadn't come out of his shell for anyone else yet at training class, but they could see his potential. Gunner is now living the life he always deserved.

Seeing how Gunner reacted to our kind interactions with our dogs was remarkable; we hadn't seen anything similar from a foster animal yet. He sensed we were nice people and that he could trust us after watching me pet our dogs in front of him. This may not work with every dog but give it a try if your foster dog needs to gain some confidence. Dogs can feed off the energy and confidence of the animals and people around them.

Meet Hoover

Hoover had the saddest face when we picked him up. Beagles have sad faces naturally, but his expression looked next-level sad. We were told his owner passed away, and he ended up homeless and at the rescue. At ten years old, he had likely been with the same owner his entire life. All he had known and the person who loved him, suddenly disappeared. The sadness he felt broke our hearts.

He did not trust us; this could be due to stranger danger, grieving, not meeting many people in his life, shock, etc. His life changed drastically, and now these random ladies were picking him up and taking him to another new place. We gave him his space and as much patience as we could.

When Hoover arrived at our house, he immediately started marking and peeing on everything. We couldn't use our go-to solution for that–the belly bands–because he would not let us near him. He darted when we attempted to put the diaper on him or even get close to him, and he nipped at Stephanie's arm once. He demonstrated this behavior out of fear; we know he didn't want to actually hurt us. Because we couldn't get the diaper on him, and our bedrooms were carpeted, Stephanie slept on the couch for his entire stay with us so he wouldn't pee all over our carpet or beds. She is one of the best people I know!

We did try to get him in a crate to avoid this sleeping arrangement, but he howled relentlessly so we gave up. Plus, our house is small so we could hear the howls no matter where we were. We didn't want to close him out of our room at night either.

When not pacing around the house, Hoover slept on the dog bed in the living room. I can't imagine how he felt trying to figure out this new environment and new people. He often seemed to be looking for his owner. Gut wrenching. It took him a solid week to calm down and settle in.

Hoover got along well with our animals from the beginning and took lots of naps. Then one day, all of a sudden, he started playing with toys. Experiencing his grief took a toll on us, so seeing a spark of happiness in his eyes and his personality come out brought us so much joy. He eventually allowed us to pet him, but only on his terms. If Hoover wanted pets, he would come over to us. If not, we let him be.

We figured we would be fostering him for a while due to his age. Older dogs tend to get overlooked and take more time to find a furever home according to the ASPCA, who reported that compared to the sixty percent adoption rate of younger dogs and puppies, senior dogs have a twenty-five percent adoption rate. Please consider adopting older dogs. They have so much love to give and deserve a great life, no matter how much time they may have left.

To our surprise, after only two weeks, the sweetest elderly lady ended up adopting him. It seemed as though Hoover felt a sense of comfort with her, too. We told her about his need for potty training and his desire to pee on things, but that didn't faze her. She loved him so much, and she went in to bear hug him immediately; his shyness didn't deter her. Something told us she wouldn't take no for an answer, and Hoover didn't seem to mind. Their adoption photo radiated pure joy and happiness. It's hard to put into words, but we just knew they were destined to be a family.

Hoover was the first senior dog we fostered. The pee problem and Stephanie sleeping on the couch aside, both of us gained a desire to keep helping senior dogs after he came through our house. His calm demeanor fit in well with our household of not so playful dogs; way less stressful than the puppy energy we've been graced with. The most challenging part, (minus the diaper debacle) proved to be helping him grieve. It just made us really sad. We focused on the fact we could offer him comfort and try to make it a little easier for him. I'm confident being with us and receiving daily love and pets made him feel better than being all alone at the rescue.

Meet Gus

A lone puppy, Gus stole our hearts right away. He resembled the chubby little mouse, Gus Gus, from Cinderella, making him even cuter. I should probably stop mentioning we don't like fostering puppies...because clearly that doesn't stop us from continuing to foster them. We are weak when puppy cuteness is presented to us.

Gus showed his intelligence quickly as he picked up potty training on day one (*phew*). He napped a decent amount of the time, usually on my chest when I laid on the couch. I tried to keep him away from our crotchety dogs whenever possible. At least on my chest I could somewhat contain him. After his brief naps, he attacked the couch pillows as if they were enemy number one. His fierceness surprised me considering his small size. He stayed with us for just five days before being scooped up by an adopter. No surprise to us! Five days proved to be the perfect amount of time to deal with his puppy energy.

"After fostering 500+ dogs over the last ten years the comment we get most is, 'oh I could never do that because I'd fall in love with all of them and want to keep them.' A bit offensive to my husband and I as it seems to imply we are heartless and don't fall in love with them or hurt when they leave our home. My standard reply to those who make this comment to us is "we definitely understand why people say this as we do hurt, love, mourn and share tears when these sweethearts leave our home but if you go visit these kill rescues and know that sweet puppy hiding in the corner of that kennel is the next on scheduled to be euthanized if a foster can't be found you too would want to take that little one home to foster and love and get vet treatment and given a chance of life.

We fosters know that our hearts will be broken when they leave our homes but we welcome the next life into our homes and do it all over again and again because the next one we bring in may be on its last day to live. Saving a life really is...all that! Please consider saving those in need. We get back tenfold the love we give saving lives."

-Brenda Brady, foster for Pet Central Helps

Meet Ginger, Killarney, Dublin, and Galway

Time to talk about poop again. A mom and her three puppies were looking for a temporary place to call home. We went back and forth with this one because it's a big responsibility and kind of a gamble. *Will the mom be protective of her puppies? Do we want to clean up poop every day again?* After some thought and discussion, we agreed to give it a try.

Ginger, a medium-sized boxer mix, arrived at our house with her three three-week-old puppies. The puppies slept most of the time the first seven to ten days we had them. Talk about "cute as a button;" they were precious! Ginger still nursed them but quickly decided motherhood might not be all it's cracked up to be. We had them all in the same room but gated off the puppies at certain times of the day to give Ginger a break from nursing. She started begging us to come out of the room and hang out with us; our dogs became besties with her right away.

Once out and about in the house, we had no challenges with her. Seriously, the best dog we've ever fostered. Ginger had the privilege of not having to go in a crate when we left; the only foster we ever allowed this for. No accidents ever. No issues with our dogs. No regrets! The best girl.

Pro tip: You don't have to crate your foster animals if you don't want to, but since you likely won't know much about them, crating them can prevent destruction or issues with the other animals in the house while you're not home. We do it for safety and precautionary reasons.

Once her puppies were weaned and no longer needed her around, she became available for adoption. While at an adoption event, the nicest lady came up to meet Ginger and fell in love immediately. She didn't bring her kids or husband to the event, so we set up a meet and greet with her family and their current dog later that week at a local dog park to make sure they would get along. It went awesome! You could tell how much they already loved Ginger which was the greatest feeling for us. They went through with the adoption, and we are now Facebook friends with them. Ginger is living a great life and is still a fabulous dog!

Ginger's puppies, Killarney, Dublin, and Galway (they arrived at our house in March so we gave them Irish-themed names; sometimes we get to name the animals if they don't already have them), were getting bigger and crazier by the day. Our daily routine with them consisted of breakfast at 7 a.m., playtime for an hour, then naptime for two or three hours in their pen. The rest of the day included more play time, dinner time, then bedtime. All three of them snuggled up together creating a cozy puppy pile. Adorable, I know.

Having each other to play with benefited us greatly. They could occupy each other, making less work for us. WWE live from the puppy room! Tackling one another never got old for them. After each nap time, they were ready to rumble again. Their pathetic little whines and cries from their pen always alerted us to their need for human interaction. Balancing spending time with them as well as our own dogs became difficult, but we managed. We told ourselves it's only temporary and we would make it work.

They slept the best at night after playing outside in the yard. The little hooligans would sprint from fence to fence and loved to chase us back and forth. Just like the other puppies that have crossed through our home, they were lots of work. There's not much else to say about puppies besides their cuteness, their massive amounts of poop, and their energy. So, I'll leave it at that.

All of them got adopted by great families, and we've been able to follow two of their pawrents on Facebook. They all have the same face as their mama. One of the coolest parts about fostering puppies is seeing what they look like when they grow up. Some of them look completely different and some look like you would expect. Regardless, it's awesome to watch them grow!

We don't have a ton of experience fostering mama dogs and puppies, but we've learned they need their own space away from your other pets. Especially when the puppies are fresh out of the womb, it's possible the mama will get protective. We didn't bring our dogs into the puppy room at all to eliminate this risk. Not to say you can't ever introduce them, just be careful. I know there are plenty of other fosters who specialize in mama dogs and puppies. Lean on them for advice if you want to learn more tips and tricks for it to be a successful fostering experience. I can connect you with some of them, too, if you're interested!

Meet Shorty

Rescuers found Shorty tied to a chain on a patch of dirt. He had a few water and food bowls, but when a volunteer went to pick him up, they found a dead rat floating in his water bowl. Put simply, he lived in bad conditions. We were a bit nervous about what his behavior would be like due to this neglect. It's hard to know how a dog will react to humans and a household setting if for most of their lives they've been tied up. He likely hadn't had much social interaction with humans or other dogs so taking him was a gamble for us.

The Humane Society explains that dogs are social creatures and need interactions from both other animals and humans. Being alone and lacking this socialization can negatively impact their physical and mental health, causing behavior issues and aggression.

Chained dogs most likely suffer from irregular and inadequate feedings. Stephanie and were nervous he could be food aggressive due to this. It's sad to think about, and we are so grateful Shorty was saved and graced our lives with his presence. Our anxiety maintained a high level when we went to pick him up; probably the most anxious we've ever been to pick up a foster dog. Thankfully, and to our relief, Shorty showed no signs of aggression and loved us from the start. His happiness and thankfulness for being saved from being chained radiated off of him. His smile beamed!

We got him home and put him right in the bath. Being a corgi mix with very thick fur, he had dirt matted into him. The tub water instantly turned brown while bathing him. We washed, rinsed, and repeated at least four times the first night. We found some ticks on him as well which is to be expected since he lived outside. Stephanie and I each pulled one off, *yuck*. We tried to have him sleep in a crate the first night; what a bust. He howled and did not want to be in there, even after we tried some classical music to calm him down. We put a belly band diaper on him and let him roam the house. Shorty slept great all night on one of our dog beds!

Shorty's crate anxiety was our biggest "challenge" to overcome with him. Most of our foster dogs aren't fond of the crate but get used to it about twenty minutes after we leave the house (we have a camera in the room to monitor them). Shorty did not calm down in his crate, no matter how long we were gone for. We kept his crate in the living room and played classical music for him when we left. We even left the TV on to see if that would help. No luck. He just howled and paced the entire time.

I hated thinking about how much he disliked being in there, but we weren't comfortable leaving him out. Sometimes he would try to get out of the crate, which made us nervous he could unintentionally hurt himself. We tried giving him CBD calming chews, which also did not work. It's hard to tell why he reacted this way in a crate. He could have had abandonment issues from being tied up, maybe he had gotten used to being free around the house and didn't like being confined, or perhaps he just missed us!

He had not gotten over this crate anxiety by the time he got adopted, which we disclosed to the adopter so they knew some crate training would be necessary.

Sometimes that can intimidate adopters, but other times they are more than willing to work with the dog. It's just a matter of finding the right home and the right person to give the dog their best life. It's best to be transparent about what the animals are working on and/or need training for. This should help the adoption be more successful. We were thrilled with Shorty's adopter. His love for Shorty shined, which warmed our hearts. From being tied to a chain 24/7 in the dirt with a dead rat in his water bowl, to living a comfortable indoor life with a human who loves him. This is a prime example of how Shorty's life went from "ruff to riches."

Shorty's crate anxiety pushed us to research and learn more about crate training, something I wished we would have done earlier. Crate training is just what it sounds, training a dog to be comfortable staying in a crate. Many rescue dogs are anxious and it's possible they could be like Shorty, if not worse. The more you know, the more prepared you'll be.

> Pro tip: We learned to start by putting them in the crate for short periods of time, maybe twenty minutes max. Leave the house and come right back. This will teach them you are, in fact, coming back and will eventually reduce their anxiety. Another tip is to take them for a long walk before leaving to wear them out. If they're tired, they may be less likely to freak out in the crate. You can also stuff a Kong with peanut butter or use a licking mat to occupy them while you're gone. This way they'll at least be stimulated for a while which can decrease their anxiety. Reach out to the rescue and other fosters for more advice if needed too. Many foster families experience similar "issues" with foster dogs that they've learned how to work through and can help you help them.

"Fostering is my way of giving back for all the blessings I have received in my life.
Helping animals find their way to their forever home fills my heart with joy. God gave us these babies to love and protect."

-Debbie Custin, foster for Pet Central Helps

Meet Leia

Leia, also known as Leia Lou and Leia Lou Who, came to the rescue with her sister, Ava. In the picture we received of them they cowered in a corner huddled next to each other. The volunteers said they were friendly, just super scared. They visibly relied on each other, and our rescue director decided it would be best to separate them for each to gain confidence. A quick note: not all dogs that come in together are necessarily bonded. They may just lean on each other because they feel safe, and sure, they're probably friends, but it's not cruel to separate them if that's what's best for both of them to thrive.

Leia, an eight-month-old sweet little lab mix had no idea what it meant to live a happy life. The volunteers were right about her being scared. Silence took over the car the entire way home. She did not whine, or bark, or really move.

When we got home, we briefly let her sniff the yard, but she had no interest in exploring. Fear froze her. Due to this fear, we did not introduce any of our dogs to her as it could overwhelm her even more. Leia needed more time to decompress.

We gave her what seemed to be the first bath she'd ever had, given the dirty water. *Maybe she had been an outside dog?* Hard to say, but she desperately needed it. Leia stiffly sat in the tub and let us get her good and clean. The warm water, soap, and scrubbing seemed to relax her. As we cleaned her up, she showed no signs of aggression toward us, despite likely being mistreated by humans all her life.

When we give foster dogs baths, they usually either freeze and let us bathe them or our bathroom looks like the inside of a car wash by the time we're done. We are always thrilled when it's the former. Leia got the deluxe wash: three rounds of soap and a rinse to get all the dirt out of her fur and tootsies.

Once sparkling clean and dry, a comfy bed, food, water blankets, and some toys awaited her in her own room. Just like we do with the others, we set a baby gate up so she could look out into the hallway but not be too overwhelmed with the other animals. Both Stephanie and I sat in the room with her for a while, but she had no interest in approaching us. We always try to remain patient, but it is difficult to not smother these dogs with love right away. We want them to know what love is, but patience is everything with scared dogs.

It's best to give them time and space to allow them to come around on their own terms. We tucked her in, and she slept great. I do think she felt safe and comfortable enough to sleep and decompress. We had not yet fostered a dog as shut down as Leia. She proved to be worse than Gunner. She would let us pet her, but she didn't really seem to enjoy it yet. At the beginning of her stay we had to carry her in and out whenever we wanted her to go potty outside. Thank goodness she allowed us to at least pick her up and that she wasn't that heavy.

On her first full day we took her outside and gave her a good brushing. *So* much hair came off her! It looked like she had her own little fluffy puppy sitting next to her. She loved basking in the sun and started to explore the yard a little bit on her own. The grass immediately freaked her out, and she didn't realize she could walk on it. Maybe she had never seen grass? It seemed very unfamiliar to her.

She would look back at us for approval and/or to make sure we were still there. Leia still stayed close to us outside and didn't go too far or explore all of the yard.

She did eventually do her business, but she would not come when called to go inside. She would just stay there, shaking. I suspect she may have been on a chain before this or in an extremely limited space. It's impossible to know exactly what she had been through, so we just use clues like these to make our best assumptions. She slowly began to make progress and even started giving us kisses.

You could see her trust in us starting to form. Fast forward to two days later, and she jumped over the baby gate to hang out with us in the living room. Quite the surprise to us, but we welcomed it ecstatically. She met our dogs and no longer had to be carried in and out to go outside. *Two days*!! Such incredible progress we were not expecting so soon. She started chewing on bones, playing with toys, getting the zoomies in the back yard, playing with our dogs, exploring the house on her own, and giving us constant kisses.

There are no words to describe how it felt to watch her transform from a terrified shell of an animal into a happy, trusting dog. We were still working on getting her comfortable around new people, though. She cowered around new people, which concerned us because we wanted her to get adopted and find a great home. We started to socialize her here and there to not overwhelm her. She met Stephanie's parents and a few of our friends, but remained skeptical around them, especially the men.

This could be because a man mistreated her in her earlier life or because they were bigger and had deeper voices. We didn't know. She made baby steps and got a little more used to strangers as time went on. We were in no rush to get her adopted, but we didn't want her to get too attached and comfortable with us and then become shut down with a new family.

We decided to start taking her to the rescue's adoption events at PetSmart. She stared at us through her crate with these big sad eyes; she got attached to us. Adoption events are great for exposure of the adoptable dogs, but it is difficult to sit there and watch our foster dogs look at us for three hours in hopes of someone wanting to meet them. A few people asked us questions about her, how she did with kids, other dogs, etc. We weren't sure how she would do with children as we hadn't introduced her to them (Louie wasn't born just yet). Due to that, we informed potential adopters her ideal home would likely be a quiet one since she remained so timid. If not a quiet home, then one with people willing to work on getting her out of her shell.

We knew she had great potential because she had been thriving at our house! Eventually, we found a family who loved her, were willing to look past her shy, scared face, and believed in her potential. Leia now has a doggy sibling and great pawrents! Her family is a foster family with Pet Central Helps, too. We love a happy ending!

Fostering Leia showed us how valuable the gift of time is when working with a scared animal. We are certainly not animal behavior specialists, but at this point in the foster journey we gathered enough knowledge and experience to know more or less what she needed. This is not to say it didn't challenge us, though.

The anxiety of wondering how she would do with a brand-new family full of different people became the hardest part for both of us. As we saw her become comfortable with us, we couldn't help but think about how much she could digress with her next family. We had to accept that yes, she probably would digress and need more time to adjust with whoever adopted her, but that's the reality of being a temporary household. We do whatever we can to help the animals while they're with us and provide adopters with as much information as possible to help everyone adjust. We also always offer our contact information should they have any future questions.

Meet Wonder

Miss Wonder was an incredibly special foster dog with a heartbreaking backstory. I have procrastinated writing this chapter because it makes me very emotional. Pet Central Helps partners with several rescues in Kentucky. Stephanie has joined a few of their Facebook pages to see what dogs our rescue may be interested in picking up and saving. While on one of their pages, she noticed Wonder. A blind, elderly dog who rescuers found roaming by herself in a ravine; probably dumped by whoever had her in their care. People suck.

Her notes said she would spin around in circles frequently and had bad arthritis in her back legs which caused her to fall down often. Stephanie said she felt pulled to foster her, so once she convinced me, we reached out to our rescue requesting they save her. Wonder had a great foster home in the state she was found, but only for about ten days. That rescue reaches out to us when they're overcrowded and need to keep their foster homes open for even more animals in need. After Stephanie's request to take her, our rescue picked her up.

Honestly, we thought it could be a hospice case. We were prepared to keep her comfortable until she passed. We set up a large pen for her with lots of blankets, a bed, stuffed animals, food, water, etc. When Wonder arrived, the rescue vet looked her over and said she suffered from vertigo, throwing off her balance causing these spins. She didn't appear to be in pain, despite the arthritis and little usage of her back legs. Overall, she received a surprisingly good report from the vet.

Her spins worsened when she became stressed out, which in turn stressed us out. We didn't enjoy watching these spinning episodes and made it a priority to keep her as stress-free as possible. We discovered that Wonder *loved* to lay outside in the sun. She romped around in the back yard looking for the perfect sunny spot; she always found it, too. She became more and more relaxed as each day passed, which made us feel better since we didn't want her to be in pain or fear. With this relaxation came reduced spins. Her quality of life seemed to be improving, and the thought of her being a hospice case faded from our minds.

It took her awhile to calm down and stop spinning when we would put her in her pen for the night, so I laid with her before I went to bed playing lullabies and petting her until she felt relaxed enough to stop spinning and fall asleep. She had a favorite stuffed animal she would snuggle up with when I left the pen. We kept an eye on her from a camera in her room, and she kept this snuggle buddy close all night.

After about three to four weeks, we posted her on the website as available for adoption.

We knew Wonder needed a particular home due to her health and vertigo. I remembered a past adopter who had adopted a senior special needs dog from another foster and friend of mine about two years prior. That dog had since passed away, so I thought maybe she would be looking for another dog. Turns out, she was! She and her family came to PetSmart to meet Wonder and ended up adopting her.

What a painful goodbye. I usually don't cry when our foster dogs get adopted. Sure, I'm sad and maybe tear up, but this adoption hit me especially hard. We had formed such a special bond, and I worried about her adjusting to another home at such an old age. *What would she do without her nightly lullabies with me? What would I do without our nightly routine?* I struggled for several weeks after she left. We considered keeping her but decided it would be too much with our other dogs.

Her adopter kept me updated frequently which gave Stephanie and I comfort as we grieved. She seemed to be doing very well with them.

Wonder lived with her family for about a year and a half when I got a Facebook message: she had taken a turn for the worse, and it was time to put her down. The family asked if Stephanie and I wanted to stop by and say goodbye. We appreciated the adopter reaching out and giving us the opportunity, but to say I dreaded that day would be an understatement. I went back and forth if I wanted to even go, but Stephanie said if we didn't go, we would regret it. So, we agreed and said our goodbyes (again) to our sweet Wonder. It was brutal. However, I know we helped give her a great last few years of life, making it worth it. Fostering can be really, really hard.

This was one of those really hard times. But ultimately, knowing we make a difference in the dog's life is why we keep doing it. We will always have a special place in our hearts for Miss Wonder.

"We all have a favorite, but then there is always one that takes an extra piece of your heart. The best decision I ever made was to fospice a chihuahua named Rita. A fospice typically comes in with a terminal prognosis and may be with you for two days, two weeks, or two months. Every single day I spent with Rita was a gift, and I got to spoil her with love and treats she otherwise wouldn't have ever been able to try (think: *real* whipped cream, chocolate ice cream, and powdered sugar donuts).

She got to experience love, trust, and companionship in her last days, and she always showed me how grateful she was. I wish she could have lived forever, but I'm incredibly thankful that she was in the arms of someone who truly loved her as she crossed the rainbow bridge. And I am forever blessed that I was "chosen" to be that person."

-Katy Green, foster for Pet Central Helps

Meet Spanky

A sad-looking, cute, little chihuahua dachshund mix? Our weakness!! Spanky came to the rescue with his brother, Max. We knew he was small and got along with at least his brother, which typically means he would be good with other smaller dogs and hopefully our medium sized dogs, too. Spanky clung to Stephanie right away.

Spanky would follow her everywhere and would only snuggle by me in Stephanie's absence. He got along great with our dogs and went potty outside ninety-nine percent of the time. Stephanie's pillow became his favorite nighttime sleeping spot (Albus did not approve of his favorite spot being taken but eventually adjusted).

At adoption events, Spanky didn't "show well." Which, yes, is a real estate term I can't help but use for multiple situations. Showing well means what it sounds like. A house shows well if it has minimal obvious problems or repairs, good curb appeal, is clean, does not need many updates, etc. A dog shows well when they are friendly, don't repeatedly bark at other people or dogs, and keep a clean crate.

At these adoption events, two rows of crates lined up with adoptable dogs in them and sometimes cats/kittens at the end of the row in cat condos. Because he could see one of us, Spanky cried and barked the entire three-hour event. Which, as you can imagine, can be a turn off to some people. It made it seem like he needed work and training which not everyone wants to take on. We took him out and walked him around, but we also wanted to make sure people who walked by could see him in his crate.

I had to fight the urge to take him out when he cried like this, but we knew he would eventually need to find a new "person," so we didn't want to keep catering to him. A young couple asked if they could take him out of his crate to meet him. We talked with them for a while as they tried to get him to warm up. Spanky didn't really want anything to do with them; they couldn't even pet him much without Spanky cowering away. New people were not his fancy. The couple didn't seem too put off by his behavior and understood he likely had a traumatic past and needed time to warm up.

They didn't decide to adopt him that day, but said they would think about it. Two adoption events later, and they decided to make him a part of their family! The best part? We found out they rented a house right across the street from us! We saw Spanky, now Ollie, all the time when out on his daily walks. He was a great watchdog for their house, too; we could always count on an Ollie bark if he saw us through the window.

He still has some anxiety and fear of new people, but his pawrents love him so much and have been willing to work with him through it. We also became friends with them, and I recently helped them find a home of their own to buy. While they are no longer across the street from us, we've remained friends and get plenty of Ollie updates. He now has a huge fenced-in back yard to run around in.

Meet Roy

We fostered Roy, a dachshund/jack russell terrier mix, about four to five weeks before our wedding (yes, we're crazy). He had a skin condition that left him with hardly any hair on his back. The rescue ran a few tests and we never found anything conclusive as to why he didn't have much hair. Roy received a good health report at the vet despite the hair loss. His previous owner, an elderly man, had passed away which is how he ended up at PCH. When Roy arrived at our house, he was a little timid, but he fit right in after a few hours and got along great with our dogs.

He seemed to be almost completely potty trained with the exception of a few turds magically appearing by the back door. For the first couple of days, he did his own thing; he didn't show much interest in toys and didn't play a whole lot with our dogs. He did love to be outside and roam around the yard, but Roy just seemed sad. I'm sure the grief of losing his owner occupied his mind most of the time. It's all he ever knew, and he had to find his way to happiness again. After about a week, he started to perk up and show signs of genuine happiness.

Like a few of our other foster dogs, one day Roy started randomly playing with toys in the living room. From a sad boy who primarily laid on the dog bed, to chasing dog toys around the living room. Watching this transformation never gets old. The time came for Roy to find his next forever family. We met a family at a local park who had put in an application for him. They had another dog and kids so they wanted to make sure it would be a good fit before adopting him. He kept his distance from them but didn't show any signs of aggression. When he came home with us, he slowly had to warm up, so we weren't surprised by this. But it can be off putting to others if the dog isn't super friendly right away, especially those who don't have much rescue dog experience.

Rescue dog experts often refer to the 3-3-3 rule, which is three days, three weeks, and three months. Amanda Guagliardo breaks down this rule in her blog "Adopting a Rescue Dog: The 3-3-3 Rule." The first three days after being adopted are the most overwhelming for a rescue dog. As they're getting used to their new home and humans, it's unlikely they'll be comfortable enough to be themselves. The dog needs to recognize they are safe, especially if they've experienced past trauma. They may not eat or drink much and may seem anxious. Just give them time; this is a big change. Make sure they have a safe space to sleep or hang out, like a crate or designated area just for them. After three weeks, you'll notice your dog becoming more comfortable in your home and with you.

You may see them start to play with toys, run around playfully, and drink and eat more regularly. Since their personality should be coming out, you may notice training could be needed. They may now feel comfortable jumping up on you or on the counter; this is a good time to start training and setting boundaries. You can start to work on sit and stay and other similar commands. After three months, your new dog should understand your home is their home, and you are their owner.

Your dog will continue building trust and confidence with you and should know what the daily routine is. This is a good time to socialize them with other people and dogs. Not to say you can't begin socializing before this point, but if your dog is nervous make sure they've had time to get used to you and/or your pets before overwhelming them with other people and animals. Roy would need plenty of time to adjust so we told his potential family about this rule.

The family decided to go through with Roy's adoption. After about a week, they contacted us and told us they needed to return him. Roy hadn't warmed up to their younger daughter and became a little growly with her. We were bummed for Roy and the family. Whenever an adoptive family decides it's not a good fit, we place no judgment on them. We know sometimes things just don't work out and that's okay. If you adopt a dog and it's not working out for one reason or another, we do encourage you to reach out to the rescue and see if they have any resources to help.

For example, we have a trainer on our staff that offers advice for helping the dog get adjusted. We also offer free training classes for dogs adopted from us. There are definitely things you can do to try and make it work. Always reach out and see if the rescue can help if you're willing to give it more time.

We brought Roy back to our house. We were of course happy to see him, despite the circumstances. He had another application come through that looked like a good fit, but it turned out the family's current dog had to undergo an expensive surgery and they no longer felt comfortable getting another dog due to the added expense.

But *then!* A sweet man who recently lost his wife applied for Roy. We met him at the rescue with Roy and immediately the adopter's face lit up. I think they both needed companionship as they grieved. Roy hesitantly approached him, but he surprisingly warmed up quicker than he had with others. I think the man reminded him of his previous owner. Some things do work out perfectly. Roy was adopted a week before our wedding; just in time! We haven't heard from his adopter, but no news is good news in our book. I'm sure they are both enjoying each other's company, and hopefully Roy hasn't left too many turd surprises around his house.

When Roy didn't do well with his first adoptive family's daughter, we realized you can't learn everything about a dog while they're in a foster home. We didn't have any children yet, so how would we know how he did with them? Sometimes, things are discovered later, like with Roy. There was nothing we could do about it, so we took him back with open arms and saved that information for the future. To learn more about them, it would be a good idea to expose them to more animals and people, big and small, if you're able.

"Being a foster dog mom has been one of the most rewarding experiences in my life. Since 2019, I have fostered twenty-seven amazing, unique, and loving dogs. Taking an animal in, showing love, providing training, and finding forever homes for them, is a chance to rewrite the history for so many precious lives."

-Ella McGowan, foster pet parent for Forever Home Dog Rescue

Meet Maya, Cate, McKinley, and Denali

We arrived at the rescue to pick up our foster dog, Maya, who had come from a hoarding situation with seven other dogs. In the crate with her sat a dog named Cate who didn't have a foster home lined up yet. Stephanie had been volunteering at intake that night and fell in love with Cate (intake refers to the night the rescue takes in a bunch of animals, gets them vetted, and ready for foster homes). Stephanie noticed Cate looked a little chubby and might be pregnant.

We had never fostered a pregnant dog before which made us think extra hard about taking Cate home. Uncharted territory and immediate panic for me. However, Stephanie convinced me to take a chance. So once again, we ended up taking two foster dogs home instead of one. Maya and Cate were both trembling, likely lacking human interaction throughout their lives so far. You would be surprised at the number of dogs the rescues take in from hoarding situations. More times than not, the dogs come in with fleas, hair loss, little weight on their bones, and fear-filled faces. These two were no exception. Both of them had tummy issues as we introduced them to a proper diet. A poop palooza yet again.

Their cuteness made up for the cleanup though. Maya, a little one-year-old chihuahua mix, weighed less than eight pounds. She warmed up to us quickly and became a clingy dog. I assume her anxiety and chihuahua personality drove this behavior. Maya either woke up in a sassy mood or a snuggly mood. Maybe she was spending too much time with Stephanie...

We preferred the snuggly side of her since our dogs did not appreciate her sassy side. She got adopted quickly by a family with little kids to keep her entertained.

As for the potentially pregnant one, Cate, we took her to the vet who said he didn't think she was pregnant, so they prepared her to be spayed that night. Once prepped for surgery however, Cate became much more relaxed, and they were able to feel little puppies in there.

This realization made Stephanie's night, but I had mixed feelings. I tried not to become too overwhelmed with the thought of the birthing process and how many puppies could be in there. My primary concern was the sheer amount of potential puppy poop in our future. I talk about poop a lot, don't I? Oh well, prepare for poop if you choose to foster. The vet estimated she would likely give birth in about two to three weeks. As we awaited their arrival, we had a maternity photo shoot with Cate. Yes, you're imagining it correctly; adorable! Her big ol' belly got bigger and bigger which brought us joy to experience.

The vet's estimated delivery timing turned out to be accurate. Two weeks after that appointment, Cate became visibly uncomfortable. We asked other fosters who had experienced a dog giving birth for advice and guidance.

"What do we look for?"

"How do we know it's time?"

"How do we prepare a place for her to give birth?"

"What if she gives birth randomly in the living room while we're not home?"

"What if the puppies aren't breathing?"

"What if I pass out?"

Can you tell I have anxiety?

Luckily, we volunteer with incredible people who helped us tremendously along the way. We set up a "nesting" area for her, which included a baby pool with plenty of blankets and a large pen over the top of it so she couldn't escape when we were away from home. We were told to pay attention when she seemed uncomfortable; pacing, panting, anything that seemed a little different than her usual behavior. When we thought labor began, I set up a few blankets, a pillow, and a sleeping bag for myself in the room right next to her pen. At about 10:50 p.m., she started randomly squatting...and all of a sudden, she yelped! My natural instinct was to run away and have Stephanie do the dirty work. I *panicked*, okay? I called Stephanie and she came in and took over. I left the room.

I worried the most about finding the heat lamp to keep the babies warm once they came out. I ran all over the house looking for it while Stephanie dealt with the nastiness occurring in the other room (I know childbirth is a beautiful thing, but I mean it's a little nasty, too). Turned out, the heat lamp was already in the room sitting right next to the crate, and I panicked for no reason (shocking, I know). One baby came out! Steph had to pop the amniotic sack full of fluid. We were told Cate should do this on her own, but if not then we should do it so the baby can breathe. Baby #1: success!

Midway through the process of baby #2, the puppy literally halfway out of the "canal," Cate decided to jump out of the pool onto Steph's lap (LOL; I was laughing, she was not) so we had to get her back in there. For this one, Stephanie had to cut the umbilical cord as well because Cate didn't chew through it like she should have. Two beautiful baby boys, McKinley and Denali.

The first four weeks of a puppy's life are typically easy. The mom cares for them completely, creating no need for us to feed or clean up after them. We just had to make sure they were extra warm and that Cate ate and drank normally. Cate had been getting pretty bad diarrhea, so we took her and her babies to the vet after about four days to make sure they were getting proper nutrition. Cate got some medications for her stomach issues and both babies got a good report. The first week went great!

Soon after, we started noticing McKinley grew substantially larger than Denali. We kept an eye on them to make sure Cate still fed both of them, but it seemed like Denali had lost interest in eating and stopped growing. It's not easy for me to write about this part of our foster experience, but Denali did not make it. It seemed to happen fast. Stephanie checked on him early one morning, and noticed he was struggling to breathe. We desperately tried to get ahold of someone at 6:00 a.m., and luckily, we got a hold of the vet and were able to meet him. But by the time we arrived at the vet, he had passed away.

We were absolutely heartbroken. With this being our first mother/puppy experience, we felt as though we had failed him. *What did we do wrong? Should we have noticed earlier?* The vet assured us nothing more could've been done by us, but it sucked. He said Denali had experienced "failure to thrive" or "fading puppy syndrome" which means there's no clear cause of death or reason that the puppy passes away within the first few weeks of life. Coming home to Cate and seeing her look around for him like a concerned mama made it all the worse. But luckily, McKinley's cuteness cheered us up a bit.

Getting to watch him grow up is one of my favorite foster experiences. Eating his first real bowl of dog food, playing with his first toy, going outside and meeting grass for the first time, experiencing his first Christmas, etc. We adored his precious little self. Cate rocked motherhood, too. That is, until after about five weeks when she appeared to be over him and ready to do her own thing, which is very common for mother dogs. We let her out with us and kept McKinley in the pen until he got a little bigger and could start going outside.

We spent lots of time with him to let him play and explore in the room, too! When he weighed enough, we took McKinley to get neutered. After picking him up, I noticed he had this cough, that I thought could be a kennel cough. Kennel cough is very contagious if dogs aren't vaccinated for it, so I called the rescue director to see if any other dogs at surgery night had it. She said no cases were reported she knew about and told me to keep an eye on him. He still had energy, so I didn't think too much of it.

The next day his cough got worse, and he had significantly less energy, so I called our director and had her listen to the cough. She told me to take him to the vet right away because it sounded like he might be struggling to breathe. I rushed him to the vet, and he discovered that McKinley had a collapsed trachea and didn't know if he would make it through the night. Just writing about this is making my chest pound; I'll never forget that long car ride with him on my lap wrapped in a blanket trying to save him. We were incredibly concerned. The vet kept him overnight in an incubation chamber with oxygen constantly flowing in.

We did not sleep much and just waited for an update. Luckily, he made it through the night. The vet had no idea what could have caused the collapsed trachea, but he survived and that's all that mattered to us.

McKinley's journey to good health had just begun. I had to give him breathing treatments every two to three hours and keep a close eye on him to make sure he continued to recover without the help of the incubator. The breathing treatments involved a nebulizer with saline solution. I also had a humidifier running on high in his room creating a constant morning fog effect; I've personally never breathed better.

I sat with him in his puppy pen all day long, trying my best to help him through this while praying he would continue to improve. Despite the physical and mental exhaustion, I would do it all over again to save his precious little life. McKinley got better and better every day with the help of treatments and antibiotics. A fantastic family adopted him, and they regularly send us updates of how he is doing and how he has grown. Going through that health journey with him made it difficult to say goodbye, although being done with the puppy poop helped a little bit. That sweet little face of his looking up at me while I gave him the breathing treatments will remain with me always. I am so glad he made it.

Now let's get back to Cate! She definitely took a while to warm up to strangers, which made us nervous about getting her adopted. Some people are patient and willing to work with scared dogs, but others aren't and that's absolutely fine. We were also concerned she had some health issues, due to what we thought were swollen lymph nodes on each side of her neck. After many negative tests and no concerns from the vet, we posted her for adoption. We were happy about her good health report but bummed we had to say goodbye soon. She had been through so much with us!

The bond created by helping a dog through puppy birth is something special. I should note that according to my wife, this bond is not one I get to claim as my own since I ran out of the room and didn't experience much of it. I don't think Stephanie will ever forget this moment or fail to mention how uninvolved I was. (I am proud to say I panicked significantly less when our baby Louie was born; probably because there were doctors and nurses in charge and my only responsibility was holding Stephanie's oxygen mask. I rocked that oxygen mask duty if I do say so myself.)

Another week went by, and Cate had no applications. At this time, we already had four dogs, a cat, and a tortoise so adopting another dog did not seem like a good idea...but not everything has to be a good idea at first, right? Yep, we adopted her! We just couldn't say goodbye after everything and decided she had to stay with us forever. She fit in great with our family and even our grumpiest dog, Bailey, liked her. I mean, c'mon!

She had to stay. We love her so much, despite her neediness and desire to get as close to your face as possible when given any opportunity. Cate is also known as: Cater Raider Space Invader and Cater Potater. No words describe her better than that. She will do anything to get pets as well as eat *everything*. Including litter box treats...gross. And she somehow maintains a great weight despite her huge appetite. Good for you girl.

This foster journey took us on a rollercoaster ride. Not only did we (and by we, I mean Stephanie) learn how to help a dog deliver puppies, but we also heavily grieved the loss of Denali. It took a while to accept we couldn't have done anything to save him. I initially didn't want to consider fostering newborn puppies again, but now after accepting it wasn't our fault, I would definitely consider it. There's no way of knowing what could happen, good or bad, and I don't want to let the fear of the unknown discourage us from helping a vulnerable puppy–or any animal for that matter–in need.

Meet Grace

Grace, a four-year-old Weimaraner, came to our house in an emergency situation. Her owner reached out and said they had to rehome her ASAP. She had accidents in the house frequently and since they had three little kids, and Weimaraners are active dogs who need stimulation, they couldn't do it anymore.

Grace was a big dog, and since our dogs don't respond well to them, we kept her separate from two of our dogs for her entire eight-day-stay. Not easy to do! It caused a great deal of stress. Plus, she hated being in her crate and broke out of it often, so we didn't feel comfortable leaving her unattended. If she broke out with our dogs in the house while we weren't home, we weren't sure what would happen. Also, we had to walk her a few times a day to keep her active and to wear her out so she would not be zooming around our house. Like I said, stressful!

Despite this stress, Grace won us over with her loving and happy personality. She just wanted to spend time with us. Being a sought-after breed, we were hopeful she would be adopted quickly, which is exactly what happened. We met her current family at PetSmart, and they fell in love. Grace has the *best* pawents! They spoil her so much. I'm Facebook friends with her mom, and I'm always seeing updates about Grace, the activities they're doing, and all the love she's getting. I couldn't be happier for her and them!

Fostering can throw a temporary wrench into your daily routine, relationships, and overall life. It is always worth it for us though. We know they need us, and we are willing to make sacrifices for them, however stressful those sacrifices may be. It's only temporary.

"If you're reading this, then it's pretty safe to assume you love dogs and/or cats! So do my wife and I. So much so, that our life isn't complete without many, many, many dogs. One of the joys in my life is helping an animal temporarily and seeing them get adopted. I love it when we can stay in contact and watch how happy their new owners are with them. There is really nothing more rewarding for me. However, sometimes circumstances dictate that a foster should join our pack for life. The rest of our pack isn't always happy about that. It takes time, and thoughtfulness to add that many animals to a pack. The biggest lesson I've learned is to be flexible.

Even when we add a new foster, I would start with the best plans of how it was going to work. I'll make them an area based on the little information that I have on them. Without fail, those plans always change! The dog or cat doesn't do well in the area I created for them. Or they need to be with someone all the time, or I don't know, any of the millions of reasons it doesn't work out. This is where watching cues and being flexible is the key to our pack's success. We do not introduce everyone at once. We are slow to introduce. We observe and proceed slowly. Not everyone gets along all of the time, but we are all a pack, and I can say without a doubt that every individual in my pack is loved and loves being a part of this family."

-Holly Hedges, foster for Pet Central Helps

Meet Tito

I know I've mentioned a poop-pocalypse, but let's talk about a pee-poca-lypse. Tito, who looked like a fluffier version of our dog Drake, had more pee in his bladder than any creature on the planet. He lifted his leg and marked *everything* he could in our house. To the creator of belly bands , bless you. You are our hero. Belly bands saved our furniture and us from cleaning 24/7. A tinkling tornado, but also a really good dog. He came from Canada too, making him our first international foster dog. Pretty cool, eh? I'm not entirely sure of the logistics of how he got from there to here; all we know is that his previous owners were moving and could not take him, so he ended up at the rescue.

When picking him up, he looked very shutdown, confused, and terri-fied. He didn't play or show much of a personality for a while. We did the slow introduction with our animals, and he did great! Timid, but tolerant. Napping took up most of his time the first week. Tito loved to be with us and find the coziest spot to nap. When a foster animal, especially one with likely not a great past, finally relaxes, it is one of the best feelings for us. It's clear they feel safe and calm with us and are decompressing from what they've recently been through. He gave us lots of kisses, constantly.

After about a week, Tito started to play with toys and our dogs in the back yard. It's always fun to see that! After he got neutered, the belly band unfortunately rubbed on his surgery wound. His leg lifting hadn't ceased yet, but we didn't want him to be uncomfortable with the belly band on. We decided to remove the belly band and wrap the bottom half of our couches in plastic wrap so he wouldn't ruin them via accidents. I should note we no longer had hand-me-down couches, so we cared a little more about them.

The things we do!! It worked though. The leg lifting and accidents eventually subsided as well, which made our lives a lot easier. Potty training is our least favorite part about fostering, but it has to be done and makes them more adoptable. We've learned some tips and tricks along the way, but are certainly not experts.

> Pro tip: Take them out to go potty every hour, and praise them like no other when they do go potty outside. Pay attention to cues that they need to go out. Whining, pacing, waiting by the door, or sniffing around are signs we've noticed.

Tito stayed with us for three weeks before getting adopted. On adoption day, we received a call from his adoptive family that Tito got out of their arms in the driveway and was hiding under their car. He would not come out for anyone and they were nervous he would run away. Stephanie and I sped to the house, which wasn't that far from us, and began to help. After thirty stressful minutes, Stephanie was able to get Tito out from under the car. The family seemed upset and nervous about this behavior from him but didn't mention wanting to give up on him.

However, Tito unfortunately did not warm up to the husband of the adoptive family, and they decided to return him.

We went to pick him up and brought him back to our house. Shortly after that, another adopter applied. She came to our house to meet him outside with her boyfriend, which made us a little nervous since Tito didn't do well with the last male in the household. To our surprise he warmed up to him quickly and the rest is history! He found his own home sweet home!

Meet Dobby

Dobby, named appropriately since he looked like the famous house elf from *Harry Potter*, stole my heart right away. Maybe it was magic... I just loved his cute and needy personality. Being younger, as in less than a year old, he had some spunk that made him even cuter. Dobby got along right away with our pack. We didn't need to give him much time to adjust. He clung to us and never let us out of his sight. Surprisingly, his potty-training skills weren't too bad either! We love that. Less pee accidents in our house always makes for a win.

Dobby had potential adopters right from the start. We loved him so much and wanted more time with him, but we also knew if he stayed much longer, we might keep him (yes, again, we're crazy). He loved to run around outside, play with toys, and give us kisses and snuggles. The sweetest little house elf ever! He made himself right at home and slept in between our pillows.

He stayed with us just for eight days, so I don't have a whole lot to write about him. Moral of the story, he was *adorable,* and I'm confident he'll be just as cute as he grows up. The family who adopted him had two small kids who surely keep him busy and entertained! We received a picture of Dobby and his new siblings playing together on the trampoline. He's a lucky little guy!

The adorable, young, smaller dogs tend to get adopted quickly from our experience. As long as they're spayed or neutered and not coughing, sick, or on medical hold, it's highly likely they may be at your house for only a short time. This is a nice way to ease into fostering if you can find a dog like this at your rescue.

Meet Sophie

Sophie, six pounds of chihuahua spunk and neediness, showed no signs of fear or nervousness when we picked her up from the rescue. She showered us with love and kisses from the beginning. These types of fosters amount to much less stress when we bring them home. When they're not shut down or scared, it's likely they won't need much time or space, if any, to adjust. However, we still do slow introductions and get to know them just in case. Sophie turned out to be an easy foster. Since she stayed with us for less than a week and brought us no "problems," there's not much to tell just like with Dobby. Two easy and quick fosters back to back, not bad!

Our dogs were unfazed by her presence and she by theirs. She fearlessly protected our back yard from those dangerous squirrels, played with all sorts of toys, and loved to go on her little walks. A woman with two other dogs adopted her right away. Sophie loves snuggling with her siblings, we are told. Her adopter also told us Sophie is her little partner and wishes she had another dog just like her.

"I love being a foster parent! I have fostered since April of 2019, and I have lost count of how many fosters I have had. I mostly foster dogs; but have fostered a few pregnant cats and some kitties. What I like most about fostering: I get to meet all these little different personalities and they are just like people...they are all different.

I fall in love with all of them! Especially the adults that haven't had it quite so good. I guess, that is why I have four foster fails... we like to call foster fortunes. The puppies are a little easier to let go; because I know they have had it mostly good and if not, at least they won't remember the bad parts. That being said it isn't easy letting them go, however, when they are adopted, I get to get some more dogs to save!

The ones that come in and are so scared and find it hard to trust us are the best to follow their progress! They love the hardest pretty quickly most of the time!

I love to get updates on all my fosters! Sometimes we don't hear anything and that is sad; but we just hope they have better lives than when we first got them!

Dogs don't live as long as we do; because they already know how to love completely no matter what, and most importantly, they know how to forgive!" This is what my middle daughter told me when our fifteen-year-old Moonie went over the rainbow bridge."

-Diana Turner Mars, foster for Pet Central Helps

Meet Malcolm

Malcolm, another chihuahua mix (totally surprising, I know), could best be compared to the shape of a little potato with the floppiest ears. We were surprised about his pickiness with food given his round shape. We tried a few different kinds of dry food, then dry food covered in chicken broth, then a mix of dry and wet food, and then just wet food.

It was the most food prep I've done since we had Lonnie. We ended up finding a recipe he liked. I forgot what the magic mixture included exactly, but it worked! Most of our foster dogs are picky with food the first day or two. It could be that they're stressed and uninterested in eating as their nerves calm, or that it's a different brand than what they're used to. I think it's more due to stress than not. Typically, after a few days they develop an appetite and decide it's time to eat.

> Pro tip: Patience is key when it comes to feeding them. We also feed them separately from our dogs. We never know how they might react since we don't know much about them. In the past, we have had some foster dogs with food aggression, but it always faded with time as they realized food is going to be a constant for them. Some dogs take longer to get past this protectiveness of their food. I recommend either feeding them separately or monitoring them while they're eating next to others to be sure there are no issues.

Once we found our inner Rachel Ray and got past the picky eating phase, Malcolm thrived. A trail of flying blades of grass followed him as he sprinted from one side of our backyard fence to the other. When not acting like the Tasmanian devil outside, he loved to hide our socks around the house. "Master sock hider" should be at the top of his resume. I found socks in random places for several weeks after he left our house and am sure some were lost forever. After his sock hiding games were over, he loved spending time with us. Not a Stage 5 Clinger though...only about stage three.

He liked his independence occasionally, which was a nice break from having a dog butt on our laps (this doesn't happen often).

We had to work through Malcolm's reaction to Albus when he passed him in the hallways. He never reacted aggressively, but he stared Albus down in a non-playful way and attempted to chase him a time or two. Due to this behavior, we recommended he go to a home with no cats. This negative reaction to our cat didn't necessarily mean he would dislike all cats, but we felt most comfortable finding him a home without them to ensure the most successful adoption outcome. However, I want to note that sometimes dogs need more time to adjust to cats or other dogs they may not like at first.

If a family is dedicated to training and helping all animals in the household adjust, it is absolutely possible they could come around. Sometimes they're just not used to other animals and introduction can take more time. It's important to remember most of these foster animals come from not-so-great backgrounds so they are working through past trauma. Don't give up on them!

Malcolm did end up getting adopted by a family with no cats which gave us peace of mind just in case he never adapted to them.

Meet Bonnie

Bonnie came to the rescue with her brother Clyde. She had a foster for a few days but needed a new foster who had more time and experience to make her feel comfortable. That's where we came in. Bonnie, a four-month-old chocolate lab mix, had absolutely gorgeous eyes. She may be one of the most beautiful dogs we've seen with her green eyes and brown coat. If you were a dog and saw Bonnie on a dating website, I have no doubt you would immediately swipe right.

Again, we took in a younger dog when we don't prefer them (seems like a lie at this point, I know), but we love helping scared dogs gain confidence, so we were in. Have you noticed we can be easily convinced? We try to avoid car dealerships.

Being so young yet shy, Bonnie likely hadn't been properly socialized as a puppy and/or been mistreated from the start. We learned from her fear how important it is for puppies to be socialized as well as appropriately trained and disciplined from a young age. Those first few weeks and months of life are crucial to their future development.

We are certainly not dog trainers or animal experts, but we've been around enough puppies to notice the signs of neglect and improper training.

Throughout the first few days Bonnie spent with us, her tail barely moved from between her legs. Just like the other scared fosters, we gave her space and let her decompress until she felt more comfortable with us. It took a solid week before she started to gain her confidence. Loud noises and sudden movements still spooked her, but she started to play and run around with our dogs. It became clear that she had the intelligence to catch onto things quickly.

She even figured out potty training quickly as the days went by. Our dogs were informed to take notes of her great behavior in the hopes they could learn something. Especially Theo, the pee monster who pees on whatever he pleases when not wearing his diaper of shame. It has become apparent that our dogs are not good note takers.

Bonnie loved our dogs and cat too! Her favorite activities were chewing on bones and chasing toys in the back yard. She received numerous applications. We wanted to be sure to reiterate to these potential families that she needed someone to continue working with her on her confidence and training due to her fears. We talked on the phone with her adopter prior to adoption to confirm Bonnie would be a good fit for them. Her adopter worked from home and had a ton of time to continue working with potty training and crate training. It worked out perfectly!

From a super shy and scared pup to a dog who enjoys adventures and hanging with her human siblings, Bonnie is evidence of how a positive environment can transform a dog's whole life.

Some would assume, like we did, if a rescue dog is a puppy, they're probably fine and friendly since they're still so young. Bonnie showed us that socialization from the start can make or break a puppy's personality. They can be as negatively impacted as an adult dog who has experienced trauma and poor socialization for years. We hadn't seen this yet before Bonnie, but now know it doesn't take long to traumatize a dog. Puppies need the same amount, if not more, proper care and TLC than any other dog does.

"Our Obie was quite the handful and required me to use every bit of energy and patience I could muster, yet melted my heart at the same time. It was somewhat magical when a solution to an issue was discovered. At eight months old, he was fearful and leash reactive (non-aggressive), territorial, and dominant.

The poor thing had constant infections in a blind eye that had to be removed, discovered during our foster to adopt trial period, and had trouble self-regulating (couldn't easily calm down). He still has his moments, and some things are still with him, but he melts into us as we pick him up to rock him, cuddle him, or just hold him to offer a sense of security around strangers coming into our house. He responds well to routine and structure, and now looks to protect (instead of dominating over) our senior dog who is five pounds."

-Debi Brownstone, foster and adopter for Pet Central Helps

Meet Mackie

The rescue Mackie originally came from had the following note on his cage card: "Does not like to be picked up." When Pet Central Helps posted pictures of him looking for a foster, they thought maybe this behavior stemmed from back or hip problems. When we picked him up on intake night, our foster coordinator Karry tried to get him in his crate as we pulled up. He did not enjoy this; we watched him growl and fight her. A potential new nickname...Mackie Attackie.

Not going to lie, seeing his reaction to going in the crate made us a little skeptical. It's always nerve wracking picking up dogs we don't know much about. *Will they bite us? Will they try to go after our dogs?* Even though we've seen the transformation process before, it's a bit stressful at first because we are essentially going in blind. Mackie was no exception! We did not hold him in our laps in the car. He seemed completely terrified and didn't make a peep in his crate the whole ride home.

Once we pulled into the garage and closed the door, we picked up his crate and put it outside in the back yard. We opened the door in hopes he would slowly come out and explore. He did not. He just cowered in there shivering with no idea of what to do or where to go. Stephanie went inside to get a can of wet food to hopefully encourage him to come out. Slowly but surely the smell of the food lured him out and we shut the crate door. We went out into the yard and called his name, but he had no desire to move from the back porch. Since he didn't like to be picked up, and we were too nervous to try, moving him became even more difficult (and frightening). His stress levels were high, and I can't imagine his reaction to being picked up by a stranger in a strange place would be a good one. Did I consider putting oven mitts on and picking him up? Yes. But let's be honest, I probably would've had Stephanie do it. She's the tough one.

After about twenty-five minutes of him quivering on the back porch, we were able to attach a leash to his collar and pull him in the house. We did not introduce any of our dogs to him; we didn't think it would be a good idea yet. He had been through enough in one day. Long van ride, medical shots, lots of handling by strangers, a new place, and brand-new people.

We set up our "pet room" and put a baby gate in the doorway. We then set up food, water and a dog bed and sat on the ground waiting for him to come to us. He didn't move or explore the room at all. We stepped out of the room in hopes that if he had alone time he would decompress. We have a camera set up in our pet room, so we kept an eye on him. Thirty minutes later we went back in to try to let him warm up to us again. He ended up getting pretty close to Stephanie, but would not let her pet him, which we were fine with. It could take a while for him to become comfortable.

He went into the crate, and we closed the door and turned on classical music for him. The quietness soon stopped, and he started crying and howling in the crate. We let him out and Stephanie slept in the guest room with him to give him his own space. We may give in too soon, but as you've read most of our foster dogs do not like sleeping in their crates the first night, or the nights thereafter. Our house is also small so we can hear their whines and howls no matter what. This may differ for you depending on your house setup. Just know the first night is typically not a restful one. It will get better though. Have your morning coffee ready to be brewed.

Slowly but surely, we introduced Mackie to our dogs, and he did awesome. They helped him gain his confidence and showed him the ropes! He started to explore the back yard and jump up on the couch with us. We were careful when we touched him because he did not like to be touched at first. Before you know it, he started rolling on his back for belly rubs. One day we noticed a large bump on his stomach; turns out he had a hernia that needed to be surgically fixed. We thought that's what could be the cause of his pain and negative reactions toward being picked up. However, even once they removed the hernia, he still didn't allow us to pick him up.

We got used to not picking him up, and it didn't cause any serious problems, with the exception of putting him in a crate as he did *not* go in there willingly. With our other foster dogs who didn't like the crate, we could at least pick them up and put them in there. But we could not do that with Mackie. Creative problem solving commenced.

I will take credit for developing the first master plan of tricking him into his crate. I would tear up pieces of cheese or lunch meat and make a sort of trail to the crate. Then, I would stick small pieces on the back wall of the crate. This mastery lasted two days before Mackie figured it out.

He started to eat all of the pieces except for the ones at the back of the crate, which meant he didn't go in there far enough for us to close the crate door behind him.

The plan needed to be tweaked.

We discovered if we looked away and pretended to be doing something else, he would eventually step far enough in to eat those pieces. I stood with my back to him, "acting" like I couldn't see him while straining my eye to look behind me from the side. At times this took several attempts. Smart little turd he was. The things we do!

We had to be quick and stealthy, but once he stepped in, we would close the crate door fast, and voila! Was I late for meetings and appointments a few times because of this task? Yep. I soon discovered I needed to allot more time to make sure I could succeed in enough time.

Mackie received a good number of applications despite his little quirk of not wanting to be picked up. And by good number, I mean three to five applications, just for reference. We had phone conversations with a few potential families, but it took a few interviews before we found the right one. The sweetest lady adopted him, and guess what? He let her pick him up right away! What a shit, but still great for them.

The foster dogs that come in terrified and need extra TLC are always the hardest ones to say goodbye to. We are so proud to see how far they've come and are thrilled they are going to a loving, furever home.

But we see them at their worst and know how much time it took to get them to where they are. It's impossible not to get attached when they grow to trust you after they've been so poorly treated in the past. Mackie's mom sent us updates which made it easier to not miss him so much.

A few months after his adoption, we received a devastating call that Mackie's owner needed to return him. She was moving to California and couldn't fly with him. Initially, we attempted to help her find a flight where she could fly with him. We called her back to discuss this, but unfortunately it wouldn't work. Due to her age, this constant going up and down the stairs made her too nervous. Plus, her new apartment was on the third floor so it would be difficult to take him outside to go potty. So, we took Mackie back and searched for a new home for him.

He had gained a *lot* of weight during his time with her, an unhealthy amount unfortunately. So, operation weight loss began. He needed to lose weight to be healthy and prolong his life.

Shortly after his return to our house, a sweet older couple, who had experience with "quirky" dogs, applied for him. After a long phone call, we invited them to our house to meet him.

> Pro tip: Inviting potential adopters to your house is certainly not a requirement when fostering. We usually do not do this, but we felt comfortable enough with them after our long conversation and thought Mackie would show best with room to run in a comfortable environment.

We all hung out in our back yard while they attempted to get to know him. They were so patient with him and were not intimidated by his unwillingness to be picked up and touched. They sat in our patio chairs for almost two hours letting him approach them here and there. He cautiously came up to them a few times, barking at them, but slowly warmed up to them and their other dog who they brought. Treats helped his confidence and curiosity of them. When they left, they decided they wanted to make him a part of their family and adopted him two days later. She texted me a few days after the adoption and told me, "He is doing awesome!"

Did Mackie's story intimidate you? It intimidated me and heightened my anxiety all over again as I wrote it. His inability to be picked up created a big challenge for us at the beginning and made us question how long he would be with us before finding the right home. When a dog has quirks like these, we know from the start it's going to take a special adoptive home. Not everyone is okay with a dog who doesn't like to be picked up. It may not physically work for them, they may have kids who don't understand that, etc. We are prepared to have these dogs for a longer time and will wait as long as it takes to find them the right home.

Meet Cheeto

Cheeto reminded me of Glenda due to his petite size and extreme neediness.

However, Glenda warmed up to us quickly whereas Cheeto feared us and took some time to come around. This fear could likely be attributed to him living in a hoarding situation all of his life. When compared to "normal" pet dogs, dogs from a hoarding situation can show significantly higher signs of fear toward unfamiliar people, animals, noises, and movements, are hesitant to being touched and picked up, have separation anxiety and attachment issues, can act out when home alone, and have more accidents in the house.

The first night he shook like a leaf continuously. We could not get him to calm down, so we kept him in a crate to decompress and went to bed. At 3 a.m. we woke up to him crying. I brought him into the guest room with me, and he cuddled with me the rest of the night. No more shaking! We also had a foster kitten at the time, Autumn (you'll meet her later), who loved to snuggle with Cheeto. Double the cuteness! I think she helped him feel a little more comfortable in our house.

Then the next obstacle arose: getting him to go outside. The outdoors terrified him, and he would run right back in when we let him out. This fear could also be from the hoarding situation if he had not been outside much or not at all. There were a lot of new noises, sights, and elements to interact with. When our dogs went outside, he would watch and raise his ears in curiosity, but it took a while for him to realize it was a safe place. He went potty in the house most of the time. Not going to lie, this frustrated us, but he didn't know any different.

We are both fairly patient people which helps with these kinds of foster dogs. We continued to help him gain his confidence and associate the outside with positive things. We brought treats outside, played with him, etc. Eventually he did gain enough confidence to go and stay outside (as long as we were in his sight of course). The potty training still needed some work, but we were sure to disclose that to his future adopter. He got adopted by someone my mom used to work with! I didn't realize the connection until adoption day but felt much better, as always, to somewhat know about the home or family he would be in.

The sad reality is there are many dogs currently in hoarding situations and many of them end up at a rescue. If you adopt or foster a dog from a hoarding case, it's important to understand they probably don't know how to be a dog. It's unlikely they've had toys or have been outside. Food and socialization were probably scarce. Not to mention human interaction is scarce. There are many resources and sites where you can read about how to help them, one of them being on my reference page. But remember every dog and household is different so do what works best for you to help them.

"I love dogs. I love small dogs, big dogs, smelly dogs, three-legged dogs, old dogs, young dogs, dogs that shed, dogs that have issues, dogs that are scared, injured dogs, dogs that have worms, dogs that have fleas, dogs that cuddle and kiss, dogs that tear up my socks, dogs that have accidents, dogs that are trained, one eye dogs, and blind dogs. I have had in one form or another these dogs in my home sometimes for a few hours and sometimes for months. This is because I'm a foster dog mom.

My first foster was a retired Greyhound Champion Racer, Anne. She was meek, mild, and scared. Anne had never been in a home or gone up steps. We gave her a place to feel safe and showered her with love. When I saw her jump into her new family's truck alongside her new greyhound siblings...I was hooked. What a rush to see the change in a dog's eyes from broken to joyful.

The last dog we fostered was a golden retriever from Turkey named Brad. This pup traveled thousands of miles to find a home and we were the lucky ones to be able to foster him. This dog was so handsome that we named him Brad Pitt and we knew from the minute we met Brad that he had already found his forever home with us.

Being a foster can be hard; loss of sleep, more hair, more slobber, and a lot of extra poop, but the rewards of seeing that pup go from fragmented to a pup that is whole again is well worth any amount of poop."

-Sue Goodwin, foster for Pet Central Helps and Good as Gold Golden Retriever Rescue

Meet Sammy Jo

Sammy Jo is sitting on my lap while I write about him to ensure I say nothing but good things. Sammy arrived at the rescue on my birthday, which made things a little tricky due to birthday plans. We had family coming to town and staying with us, so the thought of adding a foster dog to the mix sounded a bit chaotic for everyone. We were worried about him keeping our guests awake all night and not having the option of putting him in our guest room with them. Luckily another foster stepped up and volunteered to keep him at their house for the night.

As I've already mentioned but want to reiterate, a great thing about fostering is the network of other foster families willing to help out! You are certainly not in this alone, which is incredibly helpful, especially when you're starting to foster. Teamwork at its finest! This sweet one-year-old chihuahua doubled as a neck pillow and facial cleanser. Laying behind our heads became his favorite place to spend his time, and he kissed our faces until they were sparkling clean (he is cleaning my face as we speak).

The day after my birthday, I reached out to the foster who had taken Sammy to coordinate a time to pick him up. She said he got along great with all of her animals, seemed to be potty and crate trained, and appeared to be a good little doggy. What an awesome birthday gift to be getting a trained, great dog! He warmed up to me right away when I picked him up but still remained nervous. Sammy sat on my lap panting and whining, despite my attempts to pet him and calm him down. This nervous response isn't uncommon, and I never expect these dogs to be calm when they first meet us. Plus, he had been through quite a bit the last twenty-four hours. Tons of new people, places, and doggies! When we got back to our house, I let Sammy explore the back yard. He didn't want to roam around and instead sat on the deck with his ears perked listening to the symphony of our dog's barking in the house. He lived in a home with other dogs before coming to the rescue but appeared anxious to meet new friends.

We brought Cate out to meet him first; she's the most passive, so we usually use her as the ice breaker and guinea pig. Sammy wanted to run away from her as she tried to sniff his butt, but then warmed up and reciprocated the butt sniffing. They kept going around and around in circles chasing each other's butts which had us giggling. Then we slowly brought out the others one at a time, leading to more butt sniffing circles. Sammy seemed overwhelmed, but he didn't show any signs of aggression, just a bit of fear and confusion. I imagine he thought something along the lines of "Omg how many dogs are in this house?!" or "When will the butt sniffs end?!" After each of our dogs met him, we stayed outside a little longer hoping he would go potty. No luck! We headed inside.

The first couple of days Sammy had several accidents in the house. We let him outside frequently, but he didn't understand where to do his business. After fostering Sammy Jo for about a week, he appeared to be almost completely potty trained. We were so proud of him and thrilled to not be cleaning up tinkles and turds several times a day.

He did well in his crate, with the exception of a few dramatic barks and whines for the first ten minutes of being in there. His bones were his most prized possession, and he did not like when the other dogs got near them. If we or our dogs got too close when he chewed on the bones, he would get growly. This behavior could be present for several reasons, but it's definitely something that can be worked through over time with his forever family. He just needs to be productively corrected.

Since he got protective and growly with his things, we recommended he live in a home with adults and teenagers. Sammy might've been completely fine with small kids, but with his possessive behavior, it made us a little nervous. If he received an application where there were younger kids, our rescue gave us the opportunity to talk to the family and let them know of any "concerns" we may have. Some families will be willing to work through this with him and others may be turned off by this, which is completely fine. We don't judge! Families need to do what's best for them. Sammy Jo eventually got adopted by a great person with no kids. We gave her our number and she sent us an update right away; they were a perfect match.

It took a few days for my neck to readjust to losing the cutest neck pillow though, and I have yet to find such a thorough facial cleanser. Let me know if you want his number, Neutrogena.

It can be difficult to determine the "right" home for a rescue animal. Some animals make it very clear they do not like others or do not do well with children. Others make it fuzzy. We did not have children when we had Sammy Jo so we could not know if he would be good with them. That's why we wanted to personally talk to any families with children who applied. It's hard not to be picky once you've become invested in the dog's life. Go with your gut and relay as much information as you have to prospective families; both good and "bad" information is helpful as people decide to move forward. Don't hide things.

Meet Caspian

Caspian's condition and situation reminded us of Wonder's; found in a ditch, blind/spinning in circles, stressed, elderly, and in need of medical care. Another foster took him at first but felt she wasn't equipped to help him and looked for another foster home. We felt drawn to him since we had experience with this exact situation, but I hesitated since saying goodbye to Wonder tore me apart. *Did we really want to go through that again?*

But, as always, we try to put our emotions aside and focus on the fact these dogs need us. However, I want to add if hospice dog situations or extreme-need situations are not something you are drawn to, that's fine. It's a huge responsibility and will take an emotional toll on you, and it is certainly not for everyone. Stephanie wanted to take him right away and after a few discussions, we stepped up to foster.

We knew he needed lots of TLC and a calm temporary home while we figured out his medical status. He would spin in circles sometimes, but more often he would grind his teeth; we were told this could be a sign of a seizure. The rescue's vet ruled out any teeth issues and ordered a full neurological blood panel to hopefully find an explanation for the spinning and teeth grinding. The results took about two weeks, which felt like two months, to come back.

In the meantime, we noticed that as he became more comfortable and less stressed, these symptoms significantly decreased. The teeth grinding seemed to be a stress response as he only did it when overstimulated. We were sometimes able to talk him out of these episodes which gave us hope that maybe seizures were not the cause. To our relief the test results came back all clear. Originally, we didn't know if it would be a hospice situation or if he still had some good years left in him. We were so excited to know that he had a lot of life ahead of him.

Caspian, a nine-year-old white Pomeranian mix, could best be described as a fluffy little angel. He loved our dogs and cat and followed them around. I think he must've been trying to figure out where to go since he couldn't really see on his own. He also loved being outside and roaming around in the grass. Due to the blindness, if something startled him, he would "freak out." Never anything aggressive, but if we were outside and one of the dogs barked, he would rip out a pile of grass from the ground and proceed to shake it around in his mouth as if he had just caught his prey and needed to kill. We had never seen anything like this but found it hilarious to watch. What a tough guy!

We discovered more of his personality throughout his stay, such as his extreme desire to cuddle, prancing little tippy taps, and his love for his stuffed animal.

After he got used to us holding him, he would snuggle up with us on the couch every night. We couldn't leave him unattended while up on the couch or bed in fear that he could fall off since he couldn't see. For his safety, we set up a large pen for him to stay in at night and when we weren't home. We also put him in there when he got overwhelmed and needed time to decompress.

He relaxed the most when spending time outside. We could tell it brought him a lot of comfort to enjoy the fresh air; Wonder had loved her outside time too. And just like I did with Wonder, I tucked him into his bed/pen every night while playing lullabies. He would cuddle up on his bed with the teddy bear we bought him. He did not know outside meant potty time, so we needed to let him out frequently and clean his pen every day after accidents.

We went through several applications before choosing an adopter.

Caspian's ideal home needed to be with adults or older children because he did not like to be startled and preferred a calm environment. An owner with experience with special needs dogs would also be ideal, but not required. After going through applications, we found a seemingly great fit. She had Pomeranians in the past and had been looking for a dog to spoil. After she adopted him, she decided they didn't click and gave him to one of her friends. Initially, we panicked because we didn't know this person and were very protective of him due to his condition and quirks.

If you do adopt a dog from a rescue and it doesn't work out, it is highly recommended you return the animal back to the rescue so they can find another home. Rescues have a process to ensure the animals go to a safe and appropriate home. Luckily, we were able to get into contact with Caspian's new owner and she is great! She has another small dog, a fenced back yard, and is taking amazing care of him. She has contacted us a few times since with questions and updates. We are always willing to help even after adoption.

Caspian reminded us so much of Wonder which brought back both great and sad memories. I'm glad we took him in. Fostering these special and older dogs leaves much gray area. Sure, anything can happen to any dog at any time, but when you know they have medical conditions and are elderly, those chances increase. Not to mention you may not know much about said medical conditions when first signing up. After fostering both Caspian and Wonder, my worried and hesitant mindset has changed. I want to be their safe place, even if it's the last place they stay.

"At the Gunderson Senior Sanctuary, we are suckers for a gray muzzle. Senior pets come to us with an entire lived experience, sometimes with broken hearts, sometimes with some serious health issues, and sometimes just looking for a place to rest their older bones. We love being able to provide a calm environment stocked with orthopedic beds, ramps for the stairs, and plenty of soft blankets to go around. We've seen some sad seniors perk up when they felt safe and loved and become wonderful adopted family members. Fostering (and foster failing) seniors has been such a rewarding experience for us."

-Jackie Gunderson, foster for Pet Central Helps

Meet Chucky

Senior dogs are the best! Many people want puppies, which is fine, but the value of a senior dog is second to none. They are usually potty trained, don't chew things up, and their energy level is medium to low. I encourage everyone not to be discouraged by their age. It's the most selfless thing to adopt them, even though they may not have more than ten years with you. They need a furever home just like all the other dogs, if not a little bit more.

Chucky, a ten-year-old chihuahua mix, needed a furever home. We picked him up after learning he did not have a foster home and spent most of his time at the rescue in a cage. We couldn't have that! He reminded us of our dog Theo. A little grumpy, liked to sleep, but mainly super cute.

The introduction with our dogs went okay. He got a little crotchety, but honestly, if I had that many dogs sniffing my butt, I don't think I would love it either.

> Pro tip: If you have several animals, introduce the new foster animal to them one at a time. This will help them not become too overwhelmed and make it easier for you to manage should a negative reaction occur.

We monitor the butt sniffing and stay close to make sure no one gets aggressive. After he was no longer overwhelmed, he took right to our house and our pack. Chucky soon took the title of King of Naps! He loved laying on the top of the couch and swiftly stole all the dog beds in the house. He would be a prime neighborhood watch candidate as he spent most of his time staring out the window making sure no one pulled any funny business. (You can never trust those mail deliverers.) He, unlike our other dogs, could look at the window and simply observe rather than bark, at every leaf, human, and squirrel. Our dogs did not learn much from him unfortunately.

For the first week, he wanted to love us and be by us, but kept some distance. For example, he would cry by the side of our bed like he wanted to be picked up, but when we would reach for him, he would run under the bed. A bit frustrating at 3 a.m...but we knew he had likely experienced some type of abuse throughout his life that caused this hesitance so we were patient with him.

It breaks my heart when you go to pet a dog and they cower in fear. It's not easy to build trust, especially if they've experienced abuse for most of their life. But it is absolutely possible to gain their trust! A lot of patience is required but it's always worth it. After the first week, we made progress and while still a bit skittish, he finally let us pick him up without running away. That is my favorite part of fostering; breaking through that fear. It's such a special and rewarding feeling to accomplish that.

Surprisingly to us, Chucky had been on the website for about five weeks and did not have any applications. He would be perfect for an elderly person, or a family with older kids who were looking for a low maintenance dog. We thought his age could be one of the primary factors for being overlooked, but we were hopeful.

Chucky finally got adopted, but it ended up not working out due to unexpected allergies. When they returned him to the rescue, another foster stepped in as we already had another foster dog. After just another week, someone else applied for him and took him to his furever home.

If the idea of fostering a senior dog perks your interest, there are rescues that specialize in senior dogs that need foster homes. One local to the Bloomington area is Deeby's Senior Chihuahua Rescue. They are experts in senior dog care and I'm sure could always use more fosters and support. We haven't volunteered with them directly but have heard wonderful things. There are also rescues that rescue specific breeds only, for example a golden retriever only rescue. Every rescue needs help so if you find a niche, volunteer where your heart and interests lead you.

Meet Teddy

Teddy, a five-and-a-half-year-old Bichon Frise/Shih tzu mix, unfortunately had to be relinquished by his owner's family due to his owner having dementia and being permanently hospitalized. It's sad to experience this type of relinquishment first-hand and was difficult to hold our emotions back when we met them at the rescue. We reassured the family he would be in good hands, and we would find him a great home.

Teddy's owner fed him all kinds of food, including chicken nuggets, making him "thicker than a snicker" to put it lightly. Bless her heart for wanting to spoil Teddy, but this type of food is not good for dogs to eat on a regular basis. Newest Weight Watchers user activated.

Teddy loved to go on walks which made it easy to drop a few pounds. We also only fed him dog food and a treat here or there. We attempted to give him carrots as a treat, which immediately insulted him. I get it, carrots and chicken nuggets don't really compare.

Our dogs took to him right away and he to them. He also adored Stephanie and followed her around everywhere. I suspect he chose her since he viewed me as the one who tried to give him a carrot and dared to call it a "treat." Hold a grudge much, Teddy? Rude. When Stephanie wasn't around, he did enjoy hanging out with me though; mildly offensive but I'll take the runner up position. Every morning as I worked from my desk at home, he would demand to be picked up, then lay on my lap and begin entertaining me with a snoring symphony. He didn't leave my lap for hours, and his thick body usually made my legs fall asleep, but I hoped this meant we were over the carrot debacle.

Teddy had a double ear infection and didn't like ear drops; how exciting. Have you ever seen the episode of *Friends* where everyone tackles

Rachel to get her eye drops in? That is an accurate depiction of our twice daily ear drop application. If you haven't seen that episode, imagine one of us sneaking up behind him with the ear drops and the other holding him down so he wouldn't run away. This required extreme stealth, and patience, but we did it.

Teddy didn't show any signs of fear or anxiety, probably since he had been in a loving home all of his life. I do think he grieved his owner a little bit, but he adjusted quickly and enjoyed his stay with us. A family who adored the shih tzu breed adopted Teddy. He now had plenty of doggy neighbors to play with and a three-year-old human who would be his best buddy in no time.

Not many of our foster animals come from a loving home. With Teddy, we witnessed a family's heartbreak of letting their dog go to ensure he was properly cared for, as they could not anymore. Sometimes difficult decisions need to be made to place animals in new homes. We tried to be as kind as we could, and I kept one of the owner's family members informed of Teddy's journey with and after us. I hoped that brought her some peace.

Meet Rascal

Thirty-four weeks pregnant and picking up a foster dog?! Yep. We had no intention of fostering with Stephanie being that far along, but Rascal clearly needed us and a lot of TLC. (Have you noticed our "intentions" usually go to s***?) He had a skin condition that caused him to lose his fur. Medicated baths and oral medication would clear this up quickly though. We had experience with this condition from our dog Drake.

Did I mention I brought him home before checking with Stephanie? Yes. Do I recommend that? No. But luckily, she agreed with no issues. *I sure am lucky to have her as my wife.* Rascal, a less than five-pound chihuahua, would not stop shaking when we picked him up. We both took turns snuggling him in our arms to make him feel safe. No amount of snuggles reduced his trembling; we knew he needed time. We brought him home and set him in the back yard, but he darted under the patio furniture right away.

Due to this extreme fear, we didn't introduce him to our dogs right away. After setting up his pen with the foster animal usuals, like blankets, a bed, food, and water, we placed him in there to decompress. He buried himself under the blankets right away and began his sixteen-hour snooze. He woke up once or twice to eat, drink, and go potty in his pen (we just let him do his business wherever the first night since he wouldn't go outside). For a moment, the thought of him sleeping so much concerned us, but I think he finally felt safe and comfortable to rest. After his temporary hibernation, he became a much different, more confident dog. He met our dogs and cat and did awesome. Rascal also needed to have us in sight at all times or he would whine and cry. *Needy!* We didn't get annoyed by this though; from wanting little to no human touch to wanting to be right next to us was great progress. He started playing with bones and scampering around in the back yard with his chicken legs flying behind him.

We knew Rascal would be our last foster dog before our baby arrived; bittersweet since we knew it would be a while before we could foster again. Our house just isn't big enough to accommodate an additional dog on top of our current animals and a baby, not to mention the journey of figuring out motherhood with all of the animals.

While temporarily staying with us, Rascal got tapeworms. Now, we have seen plenty of tapeworms in dog poop, but these tapeworms were falling off his body in little flakes, which we *hadn't* seen before (yes, ew). They looked like little grains of rice. Do you know what also looks like little grains of rice? *Bed bugs*. Imagine the panic of an eight-month pregnant lady finding what looked like bed bugs in our bed. There were tears, fervorous cleaning, and then more tears. I'm genuinely surprised this panic didn't throw Stephanie into labor. It wasn't until we washed everything, had a pest inspector come over, and slept in our living room that we discovered it was in fact not bed bugs but tapeworms from Rascal. So, for future reference, if you see little grains of rice around your house while you have a foster dog, consult with a vet before panicking. It will save you loads of stress and a $75 pest inspector fee.

Post bed bug incident, we fell in love with Rascal fast and hard. If we didn't have a baby on the way, he wouldn't have left our house. This love for him made saying goodbye extremely difficult because we knew if the timing would've been better, we wouldn't be saying goodbye. But a great family with another small dog adopted him and we felt good about them, making it a tiny bit easier. Stephanie cried for an entire day, which could've been linked to pregnancy hormones, but we both just needed time to grieve.

Pro tip: There are several common illnesses associated with rescue animals, like kennel cough, worms in their poop (yum), and parvovirus, particularly in puppies. We have become familiar with these along the way, but I think it would be super helpful for you to do some research about them while or before fostering. Most of these illnesses can be treated with an antibiotic or ointment and are no cause for panic. Some of them require more extensive medical care, especially parvovirus. When fostering, if you notice something concerning with the animal, always consult the rescue's veterinarian team for advice and treatment ASAP. Make sure you have the rescue vet team's contact information and emergency line before you even take your foster animal home just in case.

"I think fostering is very rewarding. The best thing for me is seeing the lives we change. I will admit the challenging ones are the most rewarding though. Seeing them blossom, trust, and love is worth it all! There are times you are so proud, there are times you will cry, but the key is the good always outweighs any bad.

Foster Coordination is hard at times, there is a lot of work involved. It's being involved with all the animals, not just the ones you personally foster. There is food, general questions, detailed questions, poop, pee, potty training, good with this... good with that. I got involved when I wanted a few things better organized. They always say don't complain; get involved and make a difference. I would encourage everyone to think about it. If we all partnered together we just multiplied the benefit."

-Karry Rich, foster for and foster coordinator at Pet Central Helps

Meet Benny

Other people: "When do you and Stephanie think you'll foster again after Louie is born?"

Us: "Oh gosh probably not until he's a few years old."

Also us: *Signs up to foster Benny when Louie is three months old.*

Remember when I said in the last chapter, "Our house just isn't big enough to accommodate an additional foster animal?" Yeah...we found room.

Louie is a very laid-back baby who allows us to get plenty of sleep, so we felt ready to foster a dog way sooner than we thought. Our dogs don't seem to bother or scare Louie either, so might as well help save a life if we feel up to it. And it turns out a small house isn't always an issue when fostering.

Benny, an eight-year-old Pomeranian mix, will forever be deemed as Louie's first experience with a foster animal whether either of them remember it. Benny originally came to the rescue with his brother Bert, a four-year-old mixed breed. It became clear they didn't have a great life prior to this given their neglected conditions. Bert was nearly hairless, and both were covered in fleas. They were adopted together shortly after their arrival, but that adoption didn't work out. Back to the rescue they went.

After about a month of being there, the rescue director decided to try and separate them and see how they respond. I know what you might be thinking, isn't this cruel? As I mentioned previously, dogs that come in together may not always be bonded but instead just coexist well. For some bonded pairs, it is very obvious they need to stay together (i.e., they can't function apart) but for some they do just fine apart. Benny and Bert adjusted perfectly without one another. Bert went to a foster family who ended up adopting him, which left Benny alone at the rescue. Cue my text to the foster director that I would be picking him up shortly (after Stephanie's approval of course).

I went to the rescue to pick up a freshly bathed Benny. I picked him up and

carried him to the car. Drool and heavy breathing consumed my car ride home, which felt like it took forever. I know the stress they experience is only temporary, but it's not easy to witness it regardless. His timidness disappeared once I put him in the back yard. He sprinted around the yard smelling everything! I finally got to experience his extreme cuteness and fluffiness first-hand; he looked like a cloud.

Googles types of clouds

And not like a boring cirrus cloud, like a massive cumulus cloud. I would like to apologize to my grade school science teacher for having to shamefully look up what the types of clouds are. Anyways, as cloud boy continued to explore, he peed, and peed, and peed some more.

As I introduced our dogs to him, his favorite game to play was "you pee, I pee, you pee, I pee." After expressing himself, he kicked his back legs for at least thirty seconds straight. I sincerely wish he would've stayed with us a little longer to help me rake our never-ending fallen leaves. He wanted to claim our yard as his own.

Benny responded well to all of our dogs and even tried to play with Bailey. *Danger!* I redirected him swiftly. Bailey is becoming grumpier in her old age and is best left alone. She becomes unpredictable if other dogs try to initiate play. He desperately wanted to play but our rude dogs didn't agree. He left them alone eventually and became content with occupying himself.

A hobby of his included mocking the fire truck sirens that went off outside. We all were out in the back yard one day when I heard sirens, then all of a sudden, this piercing howl erupted from his mouth. I think I peed a little due to being so startled. After I recovered from my racing heart rate, I was able to appreciate the adorableness of it. I've never had a dog do that! It was awesome. Not sure my neighbors agreed, but to each their own.

Fostering him while having Louie created a few different obstacles but nothing we couldn't handle. Having him sleep in his crate overnight did not work since he whined a little bit, and we didn't want him waking Louie. Benny also tried to lift his leg the first day, so we needed to protect Louie's belongings from the tinkles (Theo does not have access to Louie's things either. He would absolutely tinkle on them).

Needless to say, Benny had to wear a belly band while indoors. Lastly, we didn't know how Benny would react with a baby, so we did a slow introduction and kept a super close eye when Louie played on his playmat or was in his swing. Everything went great! Our dogs also luckily didn't get protective of Louie which crossed our minds as a potential concern. Fostering while having a newborn is different than before Louie was born, but we took things a day at a time and maintained cautiousness. The adjustment didn't become too difficult.

After just four days, Benny got adopted at an adoption event. The nicest couple took him home and made him a part of their family. They lost one of their dogs a few weeks prior and were looking to save another life. They brought their dog to the event, and we all met outside to confirm everyone would get along. Sophie (their other dog) and Benny are already the best of friends, and Sophie *loves* to play with him! We are thrilled Benny got himself a great playmate in his fur sibling, and pawrents who clearly adore him. There are no nimbus clouds in his bright future.

Meet Oreo and Lulu

"Hey, ummm, I'm on my way home," I said, on the phone with Stephanie on my way home from the rescue.

"Great, I'll see you soon," She replied, unassuming.

"Could you set up the puppy pen?"

"why?"

"We're going to need something bigger than a crate." *Long silence followed by a sigh*

"Emily, what did you do?"

"Well, when I went to get Oreo she was in a crate with another dog, Lulu, who looked so sad and scared and didn't have a foster so I said I'd take them both until they find somewhere else for Lulu to go," I spit out. "Now they're both in my car."

"For the love of God. I'll go get the puppy pen."

And that's how we ended up with two foster dogs rather than one. Stephanie forgave me quickly; I am blessed. Both Oreo and Lulu wanted nothing to do with us when they arrived at our house. We don't know where they came from, but per usual, it seemed like they came from a not-so-good situation based on their fearful behavior.

After a day, Lulu started to come around. She pottied outside, sat with us on the couch, and enjoyed being around our dogs. Oreo did not. We didn't know if they were a bonded pair or not at first, but soon realized they were not. Lulu could be away from Oreo all day and didn't seem to miss her. Oreo showed only fear as an emotion and also did not seem dependent upon Lulu. Three days later, Lulu went to another foster home.

Now we were down to the one foster dog we planned for, though we did not necessarily plan for our journey ahead with Oreo. For the first time in years, I found myself researching "how to help a scared dog trust you" and "why won't my dog come near me." We had never seen a dog as scared as Oreo. If we tried to pet her, she sprinted away. She wouldn't come near us and we did not let her outside in fear she would run away under the fence and get stuck outside somewhere. She peed on puppy pads and, honestly, all over the house. Not ideal but the thought of her getting lost outside brought us too much stress, so we dealt with the cleanup. She had a nice bed and blankets in the corner of our spare room, where she spent the majority of her time, but whenever we went in there, even to say hi from a distance, she ran and hid.

We then gave her free reign of the house hoping she might get used to us and our dogs, but still, no progress. After two weeks, we were feeling hopeless, not to mention sad, as we thought of what she must've been through that made her this way. We did catch her laying on our bed a few times, but she ran away when we came near. My research of "how to help a scared dog" mainly stated to give them space and time, don't make eye contact, let them come to you, etc. Two weeks of giving space and time takes a lot of patience, a patience we were not used to with our other foster dogs. As you've read, they typically come around, at least a little bit, after only a couple of days. I did attempt to pick her up twice and snuggle her; I just wanted her to know I was nice and ready to love her. She never became aggressive; she just shook and wouldn't relax even after I pet her for several minutes. Discouraging.

Fostering these "tough" cases can be challenging in many ways, including disagreements with your spouse. Oreo caused a few arguments between Stephanie and me. I wanted to continue fostering her to see if she came around while Stephanie felt we didn't have enough time for her given that Louie took up most of our time and attention. We had numerous conversations about this throughout her stay, most of them not ending in a solution. We were able to work through these arguments, but we were both at a loss of how to help her, which caused us both stress and short fuses every now and then.

We eventually came to the agreement of giving her a month at our house to adjust and if she hadn't come around, we would look for a new foster home. I wouldn't necessarily recommend putting a time limit on a dog to make progress unless it's causing stress in your household, which is why we came to this decision.

After three weeks, we saw baby steps of progress in Oreo. We caught her playing with a bone in the middle of the night, she started jumping up on the couch (not sitting by us, but on the same couch), and she ate a piece of food out of my hand twice. I also noticed she started to follow me around, hesitantly though.

A week later, she remained at the same level of progress as the three-week mark. The month "deadline" at our house came so we had our foster coordinator look for someone else. She found an angel foster, Diana, who picked her up a few days later. Diana and her husband are retired and have much experience with reserved and shut-down dogs. Knowing Oreo was going there made us both feel better about letting her go. Plus, I know Diana will keep us updated on how she's doing. We continue to think about the animals that leave our house for long after they're here; updates help us cope. Oreo eventually found a home of her own. Her owner is willing to wait as long as it takes for her to come around.

Oreo challenged us in new ways, including putting a minor strain on our relationship. My takeaway and advice from fostering a dog like her is to be patient, communicate with your partner if you have one, and to ask others for advice. I can be stubborn and initially refused for her to go anywhere else because I wanted to be the one who helped her out of her shell. I had to realize life with a baby makes things different, and we simply didn't have the time to be those people for her, which is not an easy realization to accept.

"In the current environment, shelters are so overcrowded that fostering really saves two lives, the life of the pet you foster and the animal that can enter the shelter because you have welcomed a foster into your home. We can't change the past of the animal. Some of them have had bad experiences in the past with people and other animals. Our job as fosters is to show the animal kindness and love so that they can understand what it is to feel safe.

Things are different with a foster animal. They aren't with us to spend their lives, instead we are there to show them how to trust and how to become a pet so that they can find their forever homes. It's not just me that fosters the animals that come into my home. My pets are also an important part of the fostering process. Dogs that don't trust people often attach to my dogs before they open up to me. They learn from watching my dogs what it means to be loved, then they decide when they are ready to have that themselves."

-Jennifer Zang, foster pet parent for multiple rescues

Meet Digit

Digit, a two-year-old Pomeranian-Chihuahua mix, looked like a purse puppy and had *so much* energy. His "purse-istence" on playing with our dogs caused some stress right away. None of them liked him. And when he wanted to play, he would bark, and bark, and bark some more. This posed its own stress since we had a napping baby at times. Usually, Drake or Cate would give in and play with our playful fosters, but they were not having it this time around. We had to separate all of them for almost his entire stay with us. Cate did play with him once, but she didn't seem to embrace it that much.

Besides the stress of having to separate everyone and his barking, we did enjoy getting to know Digit. He didn't have any issues warming up to us or our household and showed no signs of past trauma, which is great! He also picked up potty training quickly; we let him out in the yard frequently, nearly every hour during the day, and he understood that was the place to do his business. The belly bands were frequently in use too though.

Digit, when not harassing our dogs, appeared to be a hoarder. He loved to find things around the house and put them under the Christmas tree. I found a sock, a carrot, an old turd (yes, poop, probably from Theo or Albus), and a dish rag under there one day. I never knew what I would find.

Digit did calm down at times and gosh was he cute, but this experience is a prime example of how sometimes it is not that hard for us to say goodbye to our fosters. We were ready for him to get adopted, because we had to separate our dogs and care for Louie. We jumped for joy at the news of an application coming in for him. His stay with us added up to nine days but felt like weeks.

He was not a bad dog, just not a great fit for our household which made us not get too attached. It's not like we weren't sad at all, but I would say for both of us the feeling of relief outweighed the feeling of sadness on his adoption day. And I think that's okay! If you have a similar experience don't feel guilty. It's normal.

Meet Milo

Milo, lovingly referred to as Pound Cake due to his shape, came to the rescue severely overweight. He should've weighed fifteen pounds, but instead weighed thirty-seven pounds. Not only did his weight put an uncomfortable amount of pressure on his joints and his body, he also appeared to be living in poor conditions due to a very bad skin infection on his under belly and groin area.

His skin was fire red and he had hair loss on his back legs. The rescue thought he may have been laying in his own pee wherever he came from, causing the irritation and hair loss. I picked him up from the rescue along with weight loss food, medication for the skin infection, and medicated shampoo.

Stephanie and I had yet to take in a dog with such a severe weight issue. *Would he be food aggressive since we would be limiting his food? Was he good with other dogs? What about kids? What if he wants to get up on the couch and bed? Do we need to get a ramp?*

Luckily, Milo did great with everything and everyone. We also bought him a nice orthopedic bed since he wouldn't be able to jump up on the furniture to snuggle for a while. (#spoiled.) The cutest part? He absolutely adored Louie. He waited outside of his nursery for us to let him in and would bark until he got his way. Mildly annoying, especially during nap time, but mainly adorable. Milo gave Louie loads of kisses. I know, precious.

He couldn't move much to meet our dogs but did catch a butt sniff here and there. He waddled through the backyard attempting to lift his leg to pee but failed. Someday, buddy! Speaking of going to the bathroom...another prime example coming of how fostering animals is not all sunshine and roses.

Due to being so overweight, Milo could not squat to go poop. There it is again, my favorite word to write in this book apparently, "poop." This squatting issue would've been less of a big deal if he hadn't had coccidia, which causes diarrhea...which ran down his behind...which had to be wiped...by me. Good thing we were fully stocked with baby wipes due to Louie. Absolutely *not* one of my favorite parts about fostering, but it had to be done. I was graced with this task the most just because I was home more than Stephanie at the time. Thinking back, I'm not sure Stephanie ever had to do this for Milo. Rude. Next poopy diaper goes to you, Stephanie. Thankfully, we took a poop sample to the vet and with medicine, this issue cleared up quickly.

Milo's strict diet only allowed for certain portions of his weight loss food and healthy treats including green beans, carrots, other dog appropriate fruits and veggies, and low calorie dog treats. First, we tried to give him green beans: immediate rejection. Next came carrots, then broccoli, then apples, then bananas. All of which he scoffed at. I made a special trip to the grocery store's produce section just to get a variety of options for him. He hated all of it.

He also did not like his weight loss food and became incredibly picky. We were somewhat surprised because we thought he'd be starving, but then figured he had probably previously eaten fast food in order to get to the weight he was at. A McDonald's McDouble or a carrot? Yeah, I understand where you're coming from, Milo.

As Milo started losing weight, he also started showing more of his personality. He loved to chew on bones and hide his squeaky toys behind the couch. He had been staying with us for almost two weeks when we noticed he suddenly stopped acting like himself. He lost his appetite, appeared to be more lethargic, wouldn't drink water consistently, and had little interest in going outside to potty. We became very concerned when he started breathing rapidly. After forty-eight hours, we and our rescue director decided he needed to go to the emergency vet. They did chest x-rays and bloodwork and suspected it was either pneumonia or something with his heart. They wanted to keep him overnight on oxygen while they figured out what was wrong. I told him goodbye and looked forward to picking him up in the morning.

I wish I could tell you Milo's story ended happily, but that was sadly not the case. We lost him. He passed away at the emergency vet that night due to cardiac arrest. There was nothing more they could do. Stephanie and I were shocked and absolutely crushed when we received the call. We didn't expect the worst. We thought he had more time with us, and ultimately a happily ever after with a new family. It's beyond difficult to write about Milo, but he deserves a chapter, even though it's not a happy one.

He was with us for just two weeks, but we love each foster animal as our own from the very beginning, so regardless of the time he lived with us, we have heavily grieved losing him. The hardest part for me to accept is that he was on his way to a better, healthier life. I had before and after videos in the works as he continued to lose weight, we had walking paths planned to take him on, and we couldn't wait to see his personality shine as he continued to feel better. And then he was just gone.

We miss him so much and it has been awful to experience his loss, but we know he felt love from us before he passed. He had a great couple of weeks at our house. He got plenty of snuggles, a comfy dog bed, relaxing baths, and all of the toys he wanted. We wanted him to officially have a furever home, so we made a donation to Pet Central Helps in his honor to formally adopt him, after which we were given his ashes and collar.

This loss is unfortunately the risk we take when we foster animals in need. Most times they do have a happy ending, but other times they don't. It sucks, but we will keep taking the risk because they need us and it's worth it in the end because they experienced our love and we theirs.

Please don't let our sad stories deter you from signing up to foster. It can be sad and emotionally exhausting, but it's also one of the best parts of our lives and we wouldn't change anything about the experience we've had thus far.

Meet Tucker

Two weeks after losing Milo, Tucker's need for a foster home came through the foster group Facebook page. He first went home with the foster director, Karry while Stephanie and I thought about it. We were still grieving Milo but decided within a few days that we would welcome Tucker, an eight year old cocker spaniel, into the rainbow zoo.

Mirroring a butterball turkey and a potato, Tucker tried to jump into my car when I picked him up at the rescue. The jump was not successful. Instead, he chest bumped the side of my driver's seat and fell back. Defeated. I picked him up and he laid right down in the passenger's seat in embarrassment.

He definitely needed to lose some weight; about ten pounds if I had to guess. I have no doubt about how he achieved his plumpness; he had a face like a teddy bear. Tucker's mooching face and patience for treats outdid Beau's, who is the food mooching king. It became very difficult not to give him more food, but we wanted him to become a healthy little lad.

Tucker has been one of the best dogs we've ever met. He had to have lived in a great home at some point. He knew shake, sit, was potty trained, knew how to play fetch, walked great on a leash, and had no issues with any of our animals. He did try to hump Beau a few times... But with correction and redirection it didn't cause any serious issues.

The only other "inconvenience" is that he couldn't jump up on the couch or bed so we had to lift him up and otherwise make sure he didn't fall off. Tucker loved to roll on his back and twice rolled right off the bed as he wasn't paying attention to where he was rolling. He was fine though. And his excessive rolling was pretty cute, especially when it didn't end in a fall.

There wasn't anywhere I could go that he wasn't right next to me. He's laying right next to me on the dog bed as I write about him. He even tried to dive bomb through the shower curtain to get to me...it went just like his attempt to jump in the car. He's a persistent little potato who became my shadow on day one.

We fell in love with him and he ended up being exactly what we needed to fill the void after losing Milo. He even had some similarities to Milo, like being a little plump, loving the orthopedic dog bed, and enjoying stuffed dog toys. Most notably, he also adored our sweet Louie. He laid right by him on his playmate, just like Milo did. I have no doubt he was meant to stay with us and help us through our grief.

I will have to leave Tucker's story open ended because he is actually the last foster animal we have right before I'm publishing this book and he's still at our house, available for adoption. It's been nearly two weeks and he's had no applications yet. Being a pure bred and being so well trained it's perplexing to us that no one has expressed interest. Maybe because he's eight? Who knows. I'm certain a lucky family will find him soon! For an update on Tucker's journey, visit my website (on the reference page) to see how his story ends.

Whiskered Away

Are you thinking, "Whoa, I cannot foster a dog. That sounds like way too much work." Or maybe, "I'm more of a cat person. Can I foster a cat?" Or maybe you like both dogs and cats and want to help both. Great! Cats are just as in need of temporary loving homes as dogs are. Stephanie and I have fostered several cats and enjoy it just as much as fostering dogs. Remember when I got mad about Stephanie adopting Albus, and now I'm *willingly* bringing more cats into my home?! I know, I know, I'm just as surprised as you are, but Albus worked his charm on me and showed me his species isn't so bad.

Fostering cats is different than fostering dogs. The process of picking them up and getting their vaccinations/shots looks similar, but the introduction and stay at our house is much different. We hardly ever introduce them to our dogs because 1) Drake may attack and 2) cats typically need more space and time to adjust than a dog. You'll read about a few exceptions to this though. You can certainly introduce them to your animals if you feel comfortable, I am of course only speaking about what we do here at our zoo.

In our experience, most of the cats do perfectly fine by themselves in our spare room with a few daily visits from us for their whole stay. We also clean their litter box daily and make sure they have food and water. Our foster cats have proven to be less dependent on us than our foster dogs, which is a big reason Stephanie and I enjoy fostering them so much. It makes for less time and work for us which is a welcome experience especially when we've fostered several dogs in a row and need a "break" but still want to help.

The bonding experience with cats has also been different for us in comparison to bonding with dogs. Since cats are less dependent, and usually not in as poor health or condition with the need of extra TLC, we don't always get so attached. Except for the kittens! We always get attached to those spunky little ninja fluff balls. I am more so referring to the adult cats, especially the ones who didn't really seem to like us. Which may seem dramatic, and Stephanie may read this and think, "huh?," but I know some of them would not accept my friend request on Facebook if given the opportunity. It's hard to explain, but some looked at me with a constant side eye as I cleaned their litter box and refilled their food and water bowls as if I was a major inconvenience to their lives.

But really, even the ones who rejected my friend request were enjoyable fosters for one reason or another. Cat fostering can be less time consuming and stressful, so if that is something you're interested in, I'd like you to meet our foster cats and kittens!

*Quick note: we fostered cats and dogs in between one another, but I wanted to put each in their own respective parts.

Meet Jan and Her Kittens

Jan, the mama cat, and her kittens (all named after characters from the show *The Office*) were our first "family" of cats we fostered. We requested a kitten condo, which is a large, tall cage with shelves that contains the kittens while we're away, so they don't get into mischief. And trust me, mischief is a kitten's specialty. If I had to describe this foster experience in three words it would be: ninjas, litter, and crazy. Kittens have *so* much energy, but boy are they cute. They get their litter everywhere and enjoy climbing on whatever they can.

Playing in their litter box (ew) and swinging from the curtains was how they spent most of their time. They would climb all the way to the top and try to jump down! They swung from the curtain to the cat tree (a true Tarzan moment), where they spent a good amount of their time. Once we got used to the energy and chaos of seven kittens, we realized how low maintenance fostering them is. They're super independent and really just need food, water, toys, and their litter box cleaned out a few times a day. Since they had each other to keep them company, they were always occupied and would wear out eventually. We enjoyed fostering them and experiencing their cuteness.

Mama Jan, a great cat and a great mama, took a couple of weeks to warm up to us as she liked doing her own thing (#missindependent). When we approached her, she never got hissy toward us, just needed time to get used to human interaction since she likely hadn't experienced much of it so far. Even though she showed hesitancy towards us, she luckily let us pet the kittens and interact with them regularly without getting possessive.

It took her a while to get adopted; sometimes older cats are with us longer because people tend to prefer kittens. After all of her kittens had been adopted, we spent a good amount of time keeping her company...although she didn't seem to care if we were in there or not.

We don't mind fostering adult cats; we just feel bad they're in a room all by themselves if they don't get along with our dogs. We attempted to introduce her to our dogs a few times, but she didn't take to them, and we didn't want to stress her out. Her time with us totally paid off! She found the *greatest* home where she is the only pet and lives a more lavish lifestyle than we do. She has all the toys and cat trees in the world, and her mom keeps us updated on how she's doing frequently. Her name is now Nancy Sinatra because she is gray with white paws which resemble Nancy Sinatra's white gogo boots.

Because cats are typically low maintenance, it's much easier (at least to me) to foster a mama cat and her kittens than a mama dog and her puppies. All you need is a spare room, food, litter, toys, and a cat condo if possible. After fostering Jan and her babies, I would absolutely do it again.

Meet the Dessert Litter of Kittens

Fostering kittens is a *blast!* The dessert litter of kittens, named after (you guessed it) desserts, came to our house when they were about five weeks old. Sherbet, Gelato, Froyo, Sorbet, Daquiri, and Custard were adorable, playful, crazy, and sweet.

A unique first experience for us was that Sherbet still needed to be bottle fed, which was surprisingly challenging but also precious. Usually, their mom teaches them how to eat regular food and weans them off of nursing. Since their mom did not come in with them (they were barn cats, so we are not sure where mom went), we had to teach the bottle baby, Sherbet, how to eat regular wet food. We quickly discovered this process required lots and lots of patience! It's important not to rush them, but also make sure they are progressing appropriately for their age. For the first few days, we bottle fed him every few hours to make sure he ate enough. Ridiculously cute, but also exhausting. A glimpse into human motherhood!

After that, we switched over to feeding him out of a syringe, trying to get him to bite at it, which is an important step in the transition to feeding him food he has to chew. *Who knew something so small could be so stubborn?* We then attempted to put the food liquid on a spoon and get him to lick it off. It only worked every so often. We always fed him near the plate of wet food hoping he would associate that area with food and eventually get him interested in the plate. After a long journey, he ate wet food one day and never looked back. We had never experienced a foster situation like this before, but we love to learn new things and will be prepared for the next bottle-feeding kitten.

Custard was lovingly nicknamed One-Eyed Wanda because she only had one eye when she came to our house. The vet prescribed her an eye ointment to see if the eye would appear and grow; it did not, so she had surgery to essentially sew the eyelid shut. This did not slow her down one bit. She still had lots of spunk, if not the most of all her siblings. I enjoyed how she "stalked" her siblings and would pounce and tackle them. All of the kittens except one were girls... *Drama!* I grew up with four sisters so had lots of experience with the female sibling drama (sorry ladies, love ya).

Drama aside, the kittens were needy and loved to snuggle. The male, Sherbet, had the neediest personality of them all. As soon as we walked into their room, they would cry like little babies. They were always so excited to see us! We had them all set up in one of our guest rooms to avoid the chaos of six kittens amongst our five dogs and cat. It's a really good set up! We kept them company a few times a day making sure they had food, water, and a clean litter box.

Once they became old enough, they were posted online for adoption and two of the orange females were scooped up right away at the weekly adoption event. Sherbet, however, had ringworm and had to stay behind. We were down to three kittens, all of which eventually got ringworm. They were then on a three-week hold before being adoptable, except Sherbet who got it first and would be done with treatment much sooner.

Shortly after, *I* got ringworm!! Not as gross as it sounds, just a circular rash that ointment cleared up somewhat quickly. You may remember getting it if you were an athlete or from a high school locker room. We had the last two kittens for a while after due to them being in quarantine. We didn't mind having them around as we were missing the others. Eventually they got to leave our house and actually got adopted *together!* (#bestiesfortheresties) We love when this happens.

"I love to foster! I mainly foster kittens because it is what works in my house. It is so rewarding to know that I am helping to save lives and bring happiness to others. The love I receive from my fosters is immeasurable and the smiles on the adopters' faces are priceless. It makes my heart happy!"

-Kelly Rutledge, foster for Pet Central Helps

Meet Bubbles

Bubbles came from a local hoarding situation where they found over twenty cats in one home, all not in great condition. She spent some time in another foster home weaning her kitten, then came to our house. Bubbles hid from us the first few days, but soon became super loving, rolling around on the floor and wanting all the attention. Once she discovered we were nice and provided pets, she became a little needy. She pawed at the door and wanted to come out and hang with us. We hadn't introduced her to any of our animals yet, and were not planning to, but we felt bad she was stuck in there wanting to come out.

We started the introductions with Albus. It did not go well. She hissed at him at first, and then lunged at him. We tried again a few hours later and she had the same reaction. Since she came from a home with so many cats, we were shocked she didn't like him. I guess we assumed she would like cats after living with that many of them. But maybe it had the opposite effect on her, and she now wanted to live without them. Who knows?

A couple days later, and after listening to her constant pawing at the door, we figured we should try to introduce her to the dogs. Rather than have the dogs come into her room and her safe space, we let Bubbles out into the hallway to explore the rest of the house and meet them. We had a baby gate up in the hallway so she didn't get bombarded with sniffing noses and so that everyone could see and smell each other while not having open access to one another. This soft intro went great, and we let her roam, cautiously and with supervision.

She *loved* dogs! She rubbed up against them purring and wanting to snuggle. Adorable! We tried to introduce her to Albus again, but the same result occurred. She lunged at him and kept hissing. Our house is small and there unfortunately isn't a ton of space to keep them separated. We were stressed she might hurt Albus (unintentionally of course, she was not a mean cat, she just didn't like him). For his safety and our sanity, we took Albus to Stephanie's parents' house. They adore him and he loves visiting there! It's definitely not ideal to temporarily remove one of our pets from our house while fostering, and we hadn't done it this far into our foster journey, but we felt it would be the best decision for this current situation until Bubbles got adopted.

When writing Bubbles' adoption bio, we put she would do best as the only cat in the home. It is possible she may get along with another cat besides Albus, but there's no way of us knowing. Based on her reaction to Albus, we figured it would be safe to mention that. I got a call from my former coworker and good friend Sue that her friend had applied for a cat on the website. Turns out, Bubbles is the cat she applied for! We love when someone we know adopts our foster animals.

We put a good word in for Sue's friend and the adoption team processed her application. Bubbles' adopter picked her up a few days later. We were so happy for her! She went to a home with two younger kids who will keep her entertained, as well as a doggy sibling who she can chase around and play with. We were also incredibly happy to have Albus back home (I'm not sure how Stephanie survived without her precious angel).

Meet Stripes

Stripes, an adult cat, is one we still get to see frequently because (spoiler alert) she ended up as a permanent resident at Stephanie's parents' house. We swapped a pregnant cat named Vivian we had been fostering with Stripes. Vivian stayed with us for only twelve hours before we realized she needed to go somewhere else. Not because of her, but because our barking dogs were causing her a ton of stress and that concerned us with her being very pregnant. We didn't want to cause her or her unborn kittens any unnecessary stress. Plus, we needed to make sure she felt comfortable and safe enough to give birth when the time came. I suppose we could've given it a bit more time to see if she calmed down, but the kittens were due any day, and it seemed that time was of the essence. She went to an excellent foster home who had tons of experience with pregnant cats.

As for Stripes, she spent nearly the whole stay under our guest bed despite our best attempts to socialize her. She did not meet any of our animals due to her timid personality, but did show signs of being sweet and loving when she peeked her head out from under the bed. She is one of the aforementioned cats who would certainly not accept my Facebook friend request, but did appreciate me cleaning her litter box and refilling her food and water bowls.

One night when we were at Stephanie's parents for dinner, we started talking about her. The next day, Stephanie's dad Ronn wanted to come over and meet her. We knew he had fallen in love when he started brainstorming potential names five minutes after meeting her. We were correct about his love for her; they adopted her, and her name is now Ziva.

They love her so much and we get to see her all the time! She loves them and tolerates their little dog Toby (aka she loves to hide then jump out and scare him). When we are at their house, she doesn't have much desire to interact with us, only coming out every so often to scope out what's going on. She is always out and about when no "strangers" are there, but isn't a fan of new people. Some cats are like that. We try not to take any offense even though we helped save her life and she wouldn't have her family if it weren't for us (you're welcome, Ziva).

"My family started fostering cats in August 2022 and quickly fell in love with it! We have one cat of our own but, as much as we love her, she very much prefers her own space. With fostering, we're getting to spend time with so many more cats. Each one has their own personality and it's so fun watching them become comfortable with us and stepping out of their shell. I am so thankful we chose to give fostering a try.

It can be sad for a moment when we say goodbye to one, but we're happy knowing they're going on to their forever home to a family that will love them, and then we get to bring in a new friend to share our home with us for a while. It's been a great experience for my kids to learn the benefits of volunteering and helping animals. They already talk about how many animals they're going to rescue when they grow up!"

-Cassie Smith, foster for Pet Central Helps

Meet Harry and Ed

This is a PSA for all the non-cat people: an unneutered cat's pee *stinks*. Like next-level stink, with the power to take over your entire house and demolish your nostrils. Harry and Ed were big ol' unneutered tomcats who resided in our spare bedroom for a few weeks. Another pair that would deny my Facebook friend request.

The stench from hell put aside, they were sweet boys and super easy fosters. So sweet and laidback, they weren't fazed by much of anything. They did intimidate me though, even after I got to know them. Their big, wide heads and thick shoulders made me think twice about approaching them. Would I trust them to have my back in a dark alley at night? Yes. Am I certain they've murdered a few mice in their past, easily? Yes. They were neutered a week after being with us and man did our nasal cavities rejoice. *Fresh air*!

They were not a bonded pair and were able to be adopted out separately. Ed, the orange one, got adopted first. Harry looked incredibly intimidating, more so than Ed, which may have deterred potential adopters. Since Harry stayed by himself in our spare room, we introduced him to our pack so he wouldn't be lonely. He did great with all of our animals, but Albus did not thrive with him around. They didn't fight or get aggressive, but Albus started losing hair due to stress. Albus's stress didn't surprise me. If I were a cat and saw Harry coming close to me, I'd either turn around or pass him and give him all of my belongings. Much to Albus's delight, Harry found a great home to call his own.

Meet Tux

Tux, named after her Tuxedo breed, loved to survey her squirrel and bunny kingdom from atop her cat tree. Before she embraced this undying love of surveying the land, the little weirdo laid right next to her litter box for a day or two. We had this huge room for her to lay in and explore and she only liked that one spot. We thought it could be because she previously spent time in a small crate and only had room to lay by her box. We weren't sure, but she didn't seem that nervous.

When we take just one cat, we're always nervous if they'll get lonely and meow and cry in the spare room when we're not in there. We didn't have to worry about this with Tux. She would meow like she needed something maybe a few times a week, usually when it had been a long period of time since we had been in the room with her. She greeted us with violent purrs as soon as we walked in. She sounded like a car revving its engine! Tux loved belly rubs, snuggling up with us, and knowing we were near, but she still enjoyed her independence.

We briefly attempted to introduce her to Albus, also a Tuxedo cat, but it did not go well. You can see a trend; maybe Albus is the problem? Stephanie's response: "NOT MY PERFECT ANGEL!! It's not *his* fault."

I don't actually think it's Albus's fault, I think cats are picky. Tux hissed at him the whole time, but we did get a few pictures since they looked similar in color (but definitely not similar in size). Their side-by-side picture looked like a before and after Weightwatchers photo; Albus being the "before".

After two weeks, Tux got adopted! We even gifted her adoptive family with the cat tree that she loved so much. We were decluttering to prepare for Louie's arrival, and we couldn't think of a better place for the tree than with its biggest fan. Tux and I's mom are Facebook friends, and I can see she is so loved (and still madly in love with her cat tree).

"Fostering cats and kittens has become the great passion of my life. I started fostering because it sounded like something fun to do. I continue fostering because it literally saves lives and brings me true joy. Taking an orphaned kitten and raising her to be a strong and sassy cat who can bring happiness and love to her adoptive home has become my life's work. I have worked with hundreds of cats and kittens at this point and am proud to say that hundreds of homes have been positively impacted because of it."

-Paige Sveda, foster for Pet Central Helps

Meet the Reindeer Litter

Do you know Dancer and Prancer, Comet and Vixen, Donner and Blitzen? Not completely accurate with the famous Rudolph song I know, but the reindeer-inspired litter of kittens were not quite up for pulling Santa's sleigh. In fact, they weren't even up for human interaction. They were found in a barn at another volunteer's house and brought to the rescue. They were feral and extremely afraid of us. It seemed like they hadn't been around humans at all in their short six weeks of life. We do not know where their mom went, which is sad but common when finding feral cats.

Once an adult cat is feral for so long, it's hard to catch them and domesticate them unfortunately. Can you imagine something twenty times bigger than you suddenly trying to pick you up and snuggle you? Hard pass. We knew they needed time to adjust to house living. We had a camera set up in their room and watched them play, then eat, then poop, then start wrestling each other again. It is cuter to witness this directly in person of course, but for about a week we could only view them from the camera.

These sweeties took a really long time to warm up; at least two or three weeks. Slowly, one by one, they were okay with us being near them and petting them. Vixen took the longest to become comfortable and still needed some time and patience when she became available for adoption. Do you remember Captain Jack? The heavy-duty Swiffer duster refill puppy? Vixen also qualified for the Swiffer duster category with her extreme fluffiness. Maybe not heavy-duty level though, likely a regular refill. She would still eliminate a good amount of dust in your home.

Eventually all of the reindeer kittens got adopted into great homes.

Vixen's adopter had experience with scared cats and helping them get adjusted; her current cat had previously been feral, so she knew the patience and time required which made us feel much better as we handed her off.

Just like with dogs, cats that need extra care, time, and patience can be more difficult to say goodbye to. There's no way of actually knowing if they're going to be okay in their next home. I used to let the "what if's" consume my mind after adoption day, and while I still wonder about them for a few days, I've gotten better at not letting the negatives and worries take over. It's out of our control and all we can do is hope for the best for them.

Meet the Fast Cars Litter

Maserati, Benz, Audi, Tesla, and Porsche moved nearly as fast as their respective car names. They were crazy! Always on the move, always tackling each other, and always climbing up our legs. Ouch. Porsche and Tesla also loved to climb up the curtains and blinds.

> Pro tip: If you foster kittens, save yourself time and frustration by removing or replacing anything you care about that they could climb up and destroy. Because they will. And quickly. Replace those items with cat trees and other cat-appropriate climbing items. Have many toys and cat scratchers available in the room too.

After we got over the shredded curtain and blinds event, they were fun to hang out with and watch play. They napped eventually too, even if for short windows of time. There's nothing better than a big pile of sleepy kittens laying on your lap. The cuteness was at its peak when they were peacefully purring in their sleep and not trying to destroy our room.

We hardly ever introduce kittens to our other animals. It makes us too nervous since several of our dogs are persnickety if not given enough space, and much like puppies, kittens don't understand boundaries quite yet. All the members of the fast cars litter were adopted after a few weeks, and by then, we were ready for a "brake" from the kitten madness.

"I love fostering kittens and young cats. So many that I've taken in over the years now live with friends and family. I find that the most rewarding part of fostering is seeing how excited the new owners are to take their kitten home. The next best part is knowing that I helped socialize and care for someone's new furbaby or best friend.

I get the joy of meeting so many new little personalities. When possible, I try to keep track of their progress and I always love seeing my "babies" all grown up and spoiled with their families."

-Jessica Rhae, foster for Pet Central Helps

Meet Autumn, Cider, and Harvest

Can you guess what time of year we fostered these three kittens? The fall, you're correct. I know, that was a tough one. Autumn, Cider, and Harvest were an easy crew of kittens to foster. They were friendly right away and loved to cuddle with us and each other. They needed no time to warm up.

The guest room they stayed in also served as my office. Kittens, understandably so, think everything is fair game to play with. Every time I went in there, my laptop had litter-dusted paw prints all over it and my printer paper appeared to be a nice object to bite. I also often found them hiding out in my desk drawers. Somehow, they got into them from the back. *Kittens are nuts.* When not in their room, I would watch them from the camera we had placed in there. They loved the dry erase board most.

I did not get much work done when in there with them. *Oh, well!* They were so curious and had to be right by me. And of course, they attacked my fingers when I dare try to type. I have email drafts saved they so kindly typed for me. #hardworkers

Here is one example for your entertainment:

8H\][NYJSLSUIEtab 4444.

It's honestly kind of impressive they used multiple keys and turned off Caps Lock?! Especially that series of 4's. Talented! I wish I could remember whose handy work this belongs to. Probably Cider.

Cider and Harvest were adopted first, leaving Autumn by herself. We seriously considered adopting her. *Could that be because we felt bad she hadn't been adopted yet? Maybe.* But she also didn't like being in the spare room alone and we pitied her as she constantly meowed for us, so we slowly introduced her to our animals. Risky...but our guilt of keeping her in there alone overshadowed our concerns about introductions. She did great with them and they with her. Albus treated her like his child and groomed her frequently...precious.

We were sure to keep a close eye on Drake, who if you remember dislikes and tries to hunt cats, especially when Autumn ran around the house. We were able to manage Drake's behavior and tried training him better, but it made us too nervous to add another cat to the mix. Drake is fine with cats ninety-six percent of the time, but Autumn was very small and it stressed us out to think about managing his behavior with two cats. We don't regret not adopting her, but man was she cute! Autumn got adopted about a week after her siblings.

I think a huge value of fostering is figuring out what kinds of animals fit into your current household if you're considering adding a permanent member. For us, we knew we could not get a kitten while having Drake. We had both always sort of thought about it, but with Drake's behavior it just wouldn't work.

Meet Binx

A young female tortoiseshell cat, Binx, darted right under the bed when we put her in our guest room. Do you notice a trend with these adult cats? It seems like most adult cats who haven't been in a home are very shy and afraid of humans. She remained under the bed for two days. When she let us close enough to pet her, she purred loudly. She loved pets on her chin, head, and cheeks.

After she got a taste of how nice humans can be and how good the chin scratchies felt, she loved to be with us and started exploring outside the depths beneath the bed. We didn't have her for long before she got an application. A couple who lived on some land with several other pets adopted her. They were so excited and not intimidated by the fact she may be nervous and hide for a few days. We were confident it would be a great match. They left PetSmart with her in her dad's arms and she looked as happy as could be.

"I think that many people don't realize how important fostering is. People have personally asked me, 'Isn't fostering bad for an animal? Wouldn't it just traumatize them before adoption by transferring to a new home?' But I think fostering is one of the best things people can do. Foster animals come into our house, either from a rescue or straight from outside, scared and confused. Animals like that, especially feral cats that people bring in, rarely have a chance. Countless animals' lives have been saved thanks to the thousands of wonderful foster homes. Once they are in a foster home, it teaches them to warm up to people, work through any past trauma or anxiety, and on top of all the other benefits, you aren't just saving that one animal, but also the animal that was able to come into a rescue, because there was an empty spot. I think Milo, one of our past independent foster cats, is a great example of why every animal needs a second (or third) chance. He came in because we were doing TNR (Trap-Neuter-Return) in the area he was found. He was a two year old grey longhaired tabby, straight from the wild. When I looked at him, I knew that he needed a chance as a pet, which I don't usually say about feral cats. After about four weeks in our home plus getting fixed and all his shots, he found a home. She was a friend of a family member, a college student with anxiety. She filled out the forms, paid the adoption fee, and walked out with a bag of cat food and her now emotional support animal. If it weren't for fostering, Milo would still be living on the streets, battling with other cats, coyotes, and racoons for food and rescue, but now, months later, he enjoys head scratches, catnip, and being the best ESA he could be."

-Jeff Miller, Midwest Strays CEO and foster

Meet Abigail and Smokey

These cats, a mother and daughter pair, were the last foster cats that came through our house. We won't foster cats until we have a bigger house since our spare rooms are now consumed by baby items. Abigail and Smokey were the most scared cats we've ever had. The others hid under beds and took a little time, but these two did not come near us throughout their whole stay. Instead, they hid in the closet or under the bed any time we were in the room.

We could see on our camera they were coming out to eat and drink and use the litter box, but only when we were not in there. They relied heavily on each other for comfort. Every time I saw them, they were snuggling. Smokey, the daughter, seemed to be a bit more confident than Abigail. She came up to us but then scurried away when we extended an arm to pet her. It seemed like she wanted to be loved but her hesitation and fear took over.

They stayed with us for a month and made maybe one percent of progress in the form of Smokey coming somewhat close to me. Both Stephanie and I were at a loss. We gave them time, space, and spent a good amount of time with them in their room. We didn't force anything and hoped they'd come around. No luck. I have no idea what they had been through to cause such fear.

We would've given them all the time they needed if we didn't need to start working on our nursery. Stephanie's due date inched closer, and we wanted to get that project done. We, in turn, no longer had a spare room to keep them in anymore, so we looked for a new foster home.

They were in that home for a while then went back to the rescue due to that foster's plans changing. I hated to think of them back there.

Not that it's a bad place, but being in a home is so much better, and I knew they would regress at the rescue. We couldn't do anything about it, unfortunately. At least they had each other.

Eventually they were adopted together, and to an excellent home! I am friends with their owner on Facebook and it seems they are making great progress there. They're still scared, even after several months, but being in the same place and getting used to it, their comfort is growing. I guess that's all they needed! More time.

Ready to Save a Life?

If I haven't convinced you to start fostering...I won't be offended. Well, not *completely,* at least. Kidding! In all seriousness, fostering animals has changed my life for the better. I know it has played a part in developing Stephanie's and my marriage as one of teamwork, communication, and patience. I've become more patient with our own dogs since all of them have trauma and I now have a better understanding of the lasting effects of abuse.

Fostering animals has also made us both better human moms, too; specifically, not being as intimidated by massive poops. (Yes, I had to talk about poop one more time.) But also we work better together as a team with Louie since we've had to divide time and responsibilities with higher need foster animals.

I again encourage you to not let the daunting and dreadful thought of saying goodbye to these animals discourage you from considering fostering. Instead, focus on the impact you can have before the goodbye. You and they will be better for it, I promise.

Without foster homes, so many more animals would be living in horrible conditions and/or not have had the opportunity to live a wonderful life. Every foster home saves not only one life, but two. One animal's life is saved by staying with you and another's by taking their spot in the rescue until they find a temporary home. It's a beautiful and necessary cycle of saving lives. One at a time.

Stephanie and I were talking the other day about fostering children, (albeit somewhat different than fostering animals) and she said something that really struck me. I mentioned I'm a little hesitant about fostering children because the thought of getting attached and potentially giving them back to the situation they came from makes my stomach hurt. She responded, "It could be brutal and sad, and it will suck, but it's not about us. It's about how much they need us."

Think of them.

Resources and Recommendations for Fostering Animals

If you have an interest in fostering animals, here's a step-by-step guide for how to get started.

*Not every rescue organization has an actual facility where they house animals in need. Some rescues rely one hundred percent on foster families and cannot take in dogs without them as they have no place to keep them. These steps likely look different based on the rescue you're volunteering for, but this is a good general list of the process.

1. Research local animal rescues in your area. Identify their mission statement and values and see which one could be the best fit for you.

2. Reach out to the rescue you're interested in via phone or email and ask them about their fostering process.

3. Fill out an application to foster.

4. Once the application is approved, ask them which animals need foster homes.

5. Identify which animal you'd like to foster and notify the rescue. If that animal isn't available, which is possible, you can pick another one or wait until one comes in that you're interested in.

6. Prepare your home: Identify a safe place for them if you have room, like a spare bedroom or room you can gate off should they

need their own space to decompress. If you don't have an entire room for them, that's okay. Just give them as much space as you can and try not to overstimulate them with multiple people and animals.

7. Coordinate a day/time to pick up the animal.

8. Pick up your foster animal with any needed supplies. For example, crate, food, toys, etc. *Some rescues will provide these supplies, and some rely on fosters to provide food, crates, etc. Ask the rescue so you know what is expected of you.

9. Ask about any vet appointments they have coming up or if they need to be spayed/neutered soon. Get the vet phone number and email should any medical issues or emergencies arise.

10. Take your foster animal home and slowly introduce them to your family! Don't overwhelm them with a bunch of new people all at once. There's a good chance they'll be scared, so slow and steady is best with minimal new faces. If you have kids, make sure they don't try to smother them with pets right away.

As I mentioned earlier, the rescue will typically provide you with the supplies you need for the rescue animals. For example, a crate, food, toys, etc. Over the years Stephanie and I have acquired items and supplies that we have found very useful to have. Here's a list of items to consider buying!

- Baby gates to section off areas of your home to give the foster animals space

- An empty tub to put their bag of food in

- Extra food and water bowls

- Old blankets and towels for the crates/pens

- A stash of cat and dog toys only for foster animals

- Large puppy pen

- Carpet and fabric cleaner

- A specific blanket for each foster dog that we can send to their adoptive home with them so it smells familiar as they adjust to their new environment

- Pill pocket treats, which helps SIGNIFICANTLY when you have to administer pills

- Dog shampoo with coconut oil to help with dry skin

- Chicken broth in case they're picky with their food

- Wet dog and cat food

- Super tasty treats to coax them if needed (soft, meat flavored treats for dog and anything tuna or fish tasting for cats)

- Dog sweaters for smaller or underweight dogs during the colder months

FAQs for the Foster Process

Here are some common questions we've been asked about the foster process. These answers are based on our experience with Pet Central Helps, so again make sure you ask these directly to whatever rescue you want to volunteer with.

Q. What if my foster animal doesn't get along with my pets or my kids?

A. If the foster isn't working out in your home, you can reach out to the foster director and they will find a new placement for the animal. Please give everyone time to adjust, though. The first day will often be a little chaotic as everyone gets used to this huge change, so don't give up right away unless there's a safety issue.

Q. Does it cost any money?

A. In my experience and from asking other rescues' volunteers, it is free or "cheap." Most rescues pay for food, medical care, grooming, toys, crates, etc. However, not every rescue operates like that. Some require foster families to purchase food or other items. It depends on how the rescue operates within their means. Ask the rescue you're interested in volunteering with all of those questions before getting started so you know everything up front.

Q. How do you pick which animals to foster?

A. In our experience, you can sign up for whichever animal you want rather than being assigned an animal. We have figured out our "types" over the years. We prefer smaller dogs, preferably fifteen pounds or less, because our medium sized dogs get intimidated by others who are bigger than them and aren't always very welcoming. Most rescues know very little about the animal when they first arrive, but they can usually test if the animals are good with dogs and/or cats. When it comes to whether or not they are potty trained, crate trained, etc., they likely do not know the answers to those questions unless the animal's owners dropped them off with an info sheet or they've been in a foster home before. Every time we bring a dog home it's honestly a toss-up on how they'll do in our household.

Before committing to a foster animal, determine what would be best for your household. For example, are you willing to pick up loads of puppy poop and let them out in the wee hours of the morning? If not, probably not a great idea to foster a litter of puppies. Do you have little kids? Are they old enough to understand boundaries with potentially scared dogs? If not, taking the most scared dog may not be the best fit. These may seem obvious but it's important to ask yourself questions like these in order for you, your family, your pets, and the foster animal to thrive.

Q. How do I introduce a new animal to my household?

A. *Slow* introduction! Don't rush anything. Even if your pets are friendly and have never had issues with other animals, you/the rescue likely know close to nothing about the foster animal. Plus, they are so overwhelmed at that point and come from not-so-good situations. They need time to adjust. Introduce them to your pets in a neutral area. Outside of your house is recommended since it's away from any of your pet's toys, foods, people, etc. Keep a leash hanging on one or both in case you need to intervene, but don't hold them back on a leash because they will feel re-strained and potentially stressed. If everything goes okay outside, bring them in but keep a close eye. Remove any of those toys and food bowls for a while so your pets don't get possessive or defensive. If it's a cat, try to give them a designated space of their own that other animals can't get to, like a spare bedroom with a gate or closed door. Cats often need slower introductions than dogs too. They'll probably hide for a few days unless they're super social. If the animal is nervous or if this is your first foster experience, like with cats, consider keeping the animals separated by a gate/door so they can sniff from a distance and decompress. Feed them on opposite sides of the gate/door too to ensure no food aggression.

Q. Does it ever make you nervous to bring these new animals into your home?

A. Absolutely! The days leading up to bringing our foster animals home, and especially the day of, we are always nervous about how they and our household of animals will adjust. It's gotten easier over time since we've had so many positive experiences, but it's still nerve wracking. My best advice would be to focus on what you can control. Don't get caught up in what could happen or over think what you will do if it doesn't work out. Take it an hour at a time. Introduce slowly. Reach out to others for support if you need it. As you have read, ninety-eight percent of the time introducing animals into our home has gone fine with a few minor hiccups along the way. You got this!

Q. Where do all of these animals even come from?

A. I'm certain it's different for every rescue, but for Pet Central Helps, we assist several rescues in rural areas of different states which are overflowing with animals in need, take from our local animal control, and also help local owners who need to relinquish when we have the room. As long as we have the room and enough foster homes, we will take animals.

Q. Do you get to name your foster animals?

A. Most of the time, no. The rescue names them when they come in if they don't already have a name. They do this to avoid duplicate names in the system if possible. However, in the instances of puppies and kittens, sometimes we do get to pick their names, like with the Irish litter of puppies. *Sidenote: when you adopt a rescue animal, you of course have the option of changing their name if you'd like. It just depends if the animal already recognizes their name or not. If they do already respond to it, it may be easier to leave it (if you like it) so they don't have to relearn a new name. Up to you!

Q. What if I fall in love with my foster and want to adopt?

A. *Yay*! This is what we call a "foster fortune." Foster families are typically first in line to adopt the animal, so let the adoption team know ASAP if you're thinking you'd like to adopt.

Q. How do you not get attached and keep them all?

A. We do get attached and it's always hard to say goodbye. I mentioned this earlier but would like to reiterate that we are but a step in their journey. If you can find it in your heart to make the sacrifice and know the goodbye is going to suck, it will literally change a life.

Q. How long will the foster animal be at my house?

A. It depends on several factors, like age, health, demand for dogs in that breed and in your area, etc. For Stephanie and I, the average is about two to three weeks for an adult dog or cat and ten days for a puppy or kitten that is already of adoptable age (which is eight weeks).

Q. What if I am fostering an animal but have a vacation planned/don't have anyone watch the animal?

A. No problem! This happens often, especially in the summer and around the holiday season. You can let the foster coordinator know you need the animal to go to another foster placement for those dates and they will make it work. The earlier you let them know the better, so they have time to figure out the details.

Q. Do you ever get nervous about your animals picking up illnesses or other things from foster animals? Like a cough, worms, fleas, ticks, etc.?

A. When we first started fostering this made us more nervous than now, but all of our animals stay up to date on their vaccines and monthly preventatives which prevents them from catching things most of the time. Maybe once or twice they've picked something up, but it was minor and they got over it fast. I remember Cate picked up ringworm and Bailey got fleas once but given the number of animals that have been through our house, I would consider that not so bad! I would recommend keeping your animals up to date on everything and giving foster animals their preventatives and any medications faithfully. The foster animals will also be up to date on all preventatives as soon as they get into the rescue's care.

Q. How often do I need to foster? Is there a certain number of animals I need to foster per year?

A. That is entirely up to you! I have yet to hear about a rescue that has a certain number of animal requirements in order to keep fostering. As far as I know, you can foster as often or as little as you want. Some people foster a few times a year while others almost always have a foster animal in their home.

Get Involved

If you are thinking about fostering, the best resources are the animal rescue and/or any current foster families. They will be able to answer your questions and go through their process with you, providing you with first-hand experience and advice. It can be overwhelming to think about, and it's certainly not for everyone, but if you are open to it, it's such an incredible and rewarding experience. Thinking back to the animals we've been able to help is one of my proudest accomplishments.

Don't let the sadness of saying goodbye deter you. I personally always dread that day, and I know Stephanie does too, but the journey is worth it. My best piece of advice is to be patient. Give them time. Even if you're not fostering but instead adopting a rescue animal, they need time. Don't give up on them because they haven't started playing with their toys yet or if they're not your snuggle buddy yet. If you have adopted an animal and were able to meet the foster family, I would encourage you to get their number or add them on Facebook to send them updates. Even a once-a-year update makes our day! We think about them more than you know and knowing they're doing great in their home keeps our mind at ease and makes us miss them a little less.

I recommend reading the Foster Resources available on the Best Friends website, mentioned on the reference page. They have great information and Q&As about fostering animals.

Another major benefit of fostering animals is it frees up space in animal rescues, allowing them to save even more animals. It is great to see the number of animals being euthanized has decreased, but there is still progress to be made. When COVID-19 hit, many families took in foster animals because they had the time due to being home more. Susanne

Kogut, President of nonprofit organization Petco Love, found that this response and the addition of foster homes proved that fostering animals could single-handedly solve the unnecessary euthanasia of animals. Susanne states that "if just two percent of pet-owning households in the U.S. fostered only one pet a year, the need for unnecessary euthanasia would be eliminated." Unnecessary euthanasia simply means euthanizing animals because there is no room for them in the rescue. I would define "necessary" euthanasia as a situation where an animal had to be put down due to health reasons, age, no quality of life left, or something unavoidable or unsolvable.

The rescue we volunteer with gets asked frequently by other rescues to help because they are overcrowded and need somewhere else for these animals to go. We help as much as we can, but we rely heavily on foster homes, so if we don't have a foster home for them or room at the rescue, we can't help. The lack of foster homes is of course not the only reason for the number of animals being euthanized, but more available foster homes would certainly continue to decrease that number.

Maybe you'll read this book and think, *this is all so inspiring and wonderful but fostering just really isn't for me.* That is okay! Fostering isn't a good fit for everyone. Maybe you aren't home enough or are someone who has a pet that needs to be an only pet. Maybe you just aren't pet savvy or live somewhere that doesn't allow pets.

Whatever the situation, fear not, there are still plenty of ways you can help at an animal rescue. It doesn't have to mean making monetary donations either.

You can donate new or gently used items, like blankets, towels, or toys. You can volunteer to walk dogs during the day. You can volunteer to help at any fundraising events they host. Maybe you are good with technology, and they need help with graphic design or website building. I cannot stress enough the difference that sharing social media posts can make for rescues as well. You never know who might catch sight of a Facebook post made by a rescue about a dog who has been with them for over 100 days. A simple share can help that dog find a home.

Here are some other great opportunities to give back and get involved.

These are just some of the opportunities that come to my mind. Each rescue will have their own specific set of jobs/volunteer positions, so coordinate directly with them for more information. No volunteer opportunity means less than another. It takes a village to save the lives of these animals.

1. **Application processor**- review applications of potential adopters to see if they are a good fit for the animal(s) for which they are applying. Consult with the foster family to see if there's any questions they can answer or a specific home they would or would not recommend. Have a conversation with the potential adoptive family to get to know them and their home.

2. **Social media marketing assistant**- help the rescue promote their animals and message via social media. Create content to increase exposure for the rescue, gain followers, and hopefully get more animals adopted.

3. **Event/fundraising coordinator**- coordinate and promote events to gain money and exposure for the animal rescue. Reach out to local businesses in the community to see if they'd be willing to host fundraisers, such as a "dine to donate" at a restaurant where the rescue gets a portion of the food sales for one night.

4. **Foster coordinator**- matching animals with foster homes is the broad definition, and I'm sure it varies from rescue to rescue. This position at Pet Central Helps includes foster home recruitment and training, processing foster applications, finding foster homes for incoming/current animals, helping manage and organize what pets will be at adoption events, and staying connected with fosters to ensure foster success.

5. **Kennel help**- clean up dog and cat kennels, refresh food and water, let animals out to go potty, organize blankets/towels/toys, give medicine, etc.

6. **Vet Help**- assist the animal rescue workers with vet needs. For

example, cuddle animals as they wake up from anesthesia after surgery, hold them while they get shots.

*May need some veterinarian background or certification for some of these tasks.

7. **Grooming**- give animals baths when they come into the rescue. Oftentimes when a large group of animals come in, they are in poor condition and dirty. We have a specific group of people who volunteer to bathe dogs and cats for a few hours that night.

8. **Adoption event volunteer**- volunteer to be a greeter, clean cages, or take photos of adopted dogs at the event.

References

Amanda Guagliardo, "Adopting a Rescue Dog: The 3-3-3 Rule," The Animal Rescue Site by Greater Good, https://blog.theanimalrescuesite.greater good.com/adopting-a-rescue-dog-the-3-3-3-rule/.

"Black Dog Syndrome: Why Black Dogs are Less Likely to be Adopted," Cesar's Way, October 9, 2019, https://www.cesarsway.com/what-is-black-dog-syndrome/.

"Chaining and Tethering Dogs FAQ," The Humane Society of the United States, https://www.humanesociety.org/resources/chaining-and-tethering-dogs-faq#bad.

Ellen Lindell, VDM, DACVB; Monique Feyrecilde, BA, LVT, VTS (Behavior); Debra Horwitz, DVM, Diplomate ACVB & Gary Landsberg, DVM, Diplomate ACVB, "Dog Behavior Problems Marking Behavior," VCA Animal Hospitals, https://vcahospitals.com/know-your-pet/dog-behavior-problems-marking-behavior.

"General Pet: Foster Resources," Best Friends: Save Them All, https://resources. bestfriends.org/general-pet/foster-resources.

Geraldine Orentas, "Fostering Pets and Why It's Important," Lake City Humane Society, June 28, 2021, https://www.lakecityhumane.org/post/fostering-pets-and-why-it-s-important.

Lauren Murphy, "What is Black Dog Syndrome?" The Spruce Pets, July 13, 2022, https://www.thesprucepets.com/black-dog-syndrome-4796374.

"The Power of Pets: Health Benefits of Human-Animal Interactions," News in Health, February 2018, https://newsinhealth.nih.gov/2018/02/power-pets.

Susanne Kogut, "Keep Fostering! It's the Solution to End Euthanasia of

Shelter Pets Today. June is National Foster a Pet Month," Linkedin, June 17, 2020, https://www.linkedin.com/pulse/keep-fostering-its-solution-end-euthanasia-rescue-pets-susanne-kogut.

"Understanding and Caring for Rescued Hoarded Dogs," Best Friends: Save Them All, https://resources.bestfriends.org/article/understanding-and-caring-rescued-hoarded-dogs.

Meet Emily

(THE AUTHOR)

Emily Buhrow is a dedicated foster animal mom, community volunteer, and real estate agent who has made it her mission to help as many people and animals as possible. Over the last decade, Emily has fostered over 82 animals, and adopted a few along the way. She is also the founder and organizer of a holiday gift drive, Presents for Residents, which ensures that local nursing home residents get a gift for Christmas. When she's not volunteering or helping people buy and sell homes, she's spending time with her wife, son, and pets (including five dogs, a cat, and a tortoise).

Learn more about Emily & pet fostering at
www.rainbowzoopublishing.com

RAINBOW ZOO PUBLISHING

www.ingramcontent.com/pod-product-compliance
Lightning Source LLC
Chambersburg PA
CBHW070107030426
42335CB00016B/2041